NEW DIRECTIONS FOR COMMUNITY COLLEGES

Arthur M. Cohen
EDITOR-IN-CHIEF

Florence B. Brawer
ASSOCIATE EDITOR

Transfer and Articulation: Improving Policies to Meet New Needs

Tronie Rifkin
University of California, Los Angeles

EDITOR

Number 96, Winter 1996

JOSSEY-BASS PUBLISHERS
San Francisco

ERIC®

Clearinghouse for Community Colleges

TRANSFER AND ARTICULATION: IMPROVING POLICIES TO MEET NEW NEEDS
Tronie Rifkin (ed.)
New Directions for Community Colleges, no. 96
Volume XXIV, number 4
Arthur M. Cohen, Editor-in-Chief
Florence B. Brawer, Associate Editor

Microfilm copies of issues and articles are available in 16mm and 35mm, as well as microfiche in 105mm, through University Microfilms Inc., 300 North Zeeb Road, Ann Arbor, Michigan 48106-1346.

ISSN 0194-3081   ISBN 0-7879-9893-1

NEW DIRECTIONS FOR COMMUNITY COLLEGES is part of The Jossey-Bass Higher and Adult Education Series and is published quarterly by Jossey-Bass Inc., Publishers, 350 Sansome Street, San Francisco, California 94104-1342 in association with the ERIC Clearinghouse for Community Colleges. Periodicals postage paid at San Francisco, California, and at additional mailing offices. POSTMASTER: Send address changes to New Directions for Community Colleges, Jossey-Bass Inc., Publishers, 350 Sansome Street, San Francisco, California 94104-1342.

SUBSCRIPTIONS cost $53.00 for individuals and $89.00 for institutions, agencies, and libraries.

THE MATERIAL in this publication is based on work sponsored wholly or in part by the Office of Educational Research and Improvement, U.S. Department of Education, under contract number RI-93-00-2003. Its contents do not necessarily reflect the views of the Department, or any other agency of the U.S. Government.

EDITORIAL CORRESPONDENCE should be sent to the Editor-in-Chief, Arthur M. Cohen, at the ERIC Clearinghouse for Community Colleges, University of California, 3051 Moore Hall, 405 Hilgard Avenue, Los Angeles, California 90024-1521.

Cover photograph © Rene Sheret, After Image, Los Angeles, California, 1990.

Manufactured in the United States of America on Lyons Falls Pathfinder Tradebook. This paper is acid-free and 100 percent totally chlorine-free.

CONTENTS

Editor's Notes

> Half of the students who begin college in America—and an even
> higher proportion of underrepresented minorities—matriculate at
> community colleges. If the bachelor's degree is a requisite for major
> social and economic advancement, then transfer must be an essen-
> tial community college mission.
>
> Cohen, Chapter 3

The effective continuation of transfer as an essential community college mission requires attention to the changing context of transfer and articulation by
those within the community college sector and those without who recognize
the important role community colleges play in providing access to higher education. The 1990s have presented a number of challenges in the transfer function
arena: decline in the transfer rate; increased public demand for accountability in
higher education; a broadening of student diversity in terms of enrollment patterns, educational, and career goals among those who seek both transfer and
employment opportunities; absence of a consistent definition of transfer and
lack of a consistent formula to arrive at transfer rates; serious reduction of budgets in education; and an expansion of interest in assessing the effectiveness of
community colleges. Based on these current challenges, efforts to improve
transfer and articulation policies and practices are critical to maintaining transfer as an essential community college mission in the 1990s and beyond. This
volume explores the issues affecting the community college transfer function
and makes recommendations for future improvements to the transfer and articulation process.

Chapter One is devoted to a historical perspective of transfer and articulation. Kintzer discusses the rise of the transfer function and how the relationship
between articulation and transfer became more important as two-year colleges
received more attention and expanded their services. In addition, the chapter
speculates on the trends in articulation and transfer leading into the next century. With Chapter Two the volume moves to the present and the authors,
Robertson and Frier, focus on the role of the state in transfer and articulation.
The question is not whether states will be more aggressive in promoting transfer and articulation in higher education, but how soon, how much, in what
form, and for whom. Failure on the part of some colleges and universities to
work closely together has created a vacuum that is being filled by state mandates. The authors discuss the reasons for the new state commitment and the
arenas in which states are involved in transfer and articulation.

The discussion turns from the state to the local perspective. In Chapter
Three, Cohen discusses the results of a study that explores transfer as a function

of college activities and the perceptions held by students, faculty, administrators, and staff. This chapter presents differences in college policies, history, and staff and student attitudes between high and low transfer rate colleges in the same state. Laanan and Sanchez, the authors of Chapter Four, look at the controversies involved in measuring transfer rates and introduce new ways of conceptualizing transfer rates. The alternative definitions of transfer they present are designed to more accurately measure the community college's contribution to students' progress toward the baccalaureate. Spicer and Armstrong, in Chapter Five, explore further the controversy over transfer rate definitions and formulas by demonstrating how the transfer rate can vary depending on the criteria used to determine which students to consider in the potential pool of transfer students.

Chapters Six and Seven return us to the importance of articulation in the transfer function. In Chapter Six, articulation is presented in the context of the changing transfer student population. The transfer student population has been enlarged primarily by nontraditional students such as displaced workers, those with career or technical training who need upgrading, welfare recipients who require vocational skills training, and women reentering higher education after a hiatus. These individuals deserve opportunities to transfer and Knoell argues that a collaborative model of articulation is one viable approach to accommodating these students. She presents a number of innovative approaches to collaboration. Palmer, in Chapter Seven, takes the argument one step further and suggests that because curriculum is the key to articulation, collaboration between two- and four-year institutions can be neither effective nor successful without continual two- and four-year faculty deliberations.

In Chapter Eight I attempt to expand on the preceding chapters by drawing implications for the practice of transfer and articulation policy. Finally, in Chapter Nine, Burstein draws from the ERIC database literature to supplement the text and to provide examples of the ways in which community colleges are confronting these challenges and meeting the new needs of transfer and articulation.

In closing, I would like to note that interest in creating this volume on transfer and articulation was spawned at a two-day conference, *Transfer for the Twenty-First Century,* sponsored by the University of Arizona's Center for Transfer Students in February 1995, at which the majority of the authors in this volume presented their views on transfer and articulation in community colleges—current and future.

Tronie Rifkin
Editor

TRONIE RIFKIN is publications coordinator at the ERIC Clearinghouse for Community Colleges and a doctoral candidate in higher education at the Graduate School of Education and Information Studies, University of California, Los Angeles.

*The author presents a history of articulation and transfer by
highlighting the important research works for each period and
speculating on the policy trends and practices in these areas as they
have been shaped by history.*

A Historical and Futuristic Perspective of Articulation and Transfer in the United States

Frederick C. Kintzer

Articulation and transfer have been given many definitions. Collaborative efforts
among schools and colleges and mutual understanding among key leaders are
common threads dominating various interpretations [see Menacker (1975) and
the American Council on Education *Guidelines for Improving Articulation Between
Community/Junior and Senior Colleges* (1983) for comprehensive statements]. The
following interpretations of the two key words, *articulation* and *transfer*, are
offered to clarify the meaning of the words as repeated in the literature. Articulation is viewed as the totality of services for students transferring throughout
higher education, and transfer depicts the formulas developed to exchange credits, courses, and curriculums. For more than twenty-eight years I have used the
word *articulation* to refer to the development of a variety of procedures designed
to provide a continuous smooth flow of students, that is, all kinds of *transfers*—
vertical and horizontal, from grade to grade, and school to school.

In persisting over the years with these interpretations, I continue to stress
the importance of attitude—commitment to the total process—"the willingness or reluctance of responsible people to enter voluntarily into cooperative
planning agreements, placing the student ahead of administrative expediency"
(Kintzer, 1973, p. 2). As responsibility for developing articulation and transfer policies continues to expand into political arenas involving many types of
quasi-educational institutions and organizations, a positive attitude and willingness to collaborate remains critically important. Sacrificing or compromis-
ing an institutional advantage is sometimes necessary to maintain a fair and
flexible articulation and transfer system.

Historiography of Articulation and Transfer: The Early Decades

The story of articulation and transfer covers most of this century, beginning with well-known personalities William Rainey Harper (as early as 1903), Charles McLane (1913), Alexis Lange (1916), and James Angell (1917) speaking and writing about the junior college as a part of the public school system. Virtually all early scholars, except Leonard Koos, Walter Eells, and Floyd McDowell, concentrated almost entirely on the organization of the junior college. Were these new institutions elongated high schools, decapitated small colleges, or amputated senior colleges? By 1896, Harper had divided the undergraduate program of the University of Chicago into senior and junior college divisions, presaging transfer. Harper, in his prolific writing and lecturing, promoted the six-four-four plan. Angell, McLane, and other educational leaders of the day also preferred the upward extension pattern. Koos's book, *Integrating High School and College: The Six-Four-Four Plan at Work* (1946), is the definitive statement on upper-extension.

As early as 1907, a fascinating program was started by the University of California, Berkeley to encourage high schools to provide college-level classes. Junior certificates authorizing completion of the first two years at University of California at Berkeley (UCB) were awarded. Students could complete up to forty-five units in high school, marking the distinction between secondary and university education. By 1915, some fifty students had transferred to UCB from five extended high schools. The university continued these affiliated arrangements until 1926. State legislation, dating 1921, gave legal status to this innovative program, perhaps the earliest of its type.

The writings of Koos beginning in 1922 dominated the early scene. His classic two-volume work, *The Junior College* (1924) strongly influenced the development of junior-senior college relations. Research on the success of junior college graduates moving into universities was first presented by Koos in his written works. He found that junior college students perform equally as well as native university students.

In the early decades, the transfer function was a comparatively simple enterprise confined almost entirely to the vertical transfer of high school graduates to junior colleges to universities. As clearly summarized in the recent work of Witt, Wattenbarger, Gollattscheck, and Suppiger (1994), both the transfer and terminal objectives of the early junior colleges were in place and functioning. The early junior colleges were viewed from an organizational perspective as extensions of high schools—part collegiate, part vocational—and terminal. In actual operation, the collegiate function was limited to vertical transfer.

McDowell's dissertation, completed in 1918 at the University of Iowa, was the first national study of junior colleges and the collegiate function. Although reasons for the existence of junior colleges dominate McDowell's research, he suggests that the collegiate function, defined as "meeting the entrance requirements of professional schools," was rated in the middle range of responses by public junior college administrators (McDowell, 1919, in Eells, 1931, pp. 289–318).

The early decades also saw the establishment of national commissions, private organizations, and accrediting associations, drawing further attention to articulation and transfer. The earliest of these influential groups was the NEA-appointed Committee on Secondary School Studies, popularly known as the Committee of Ten. One of the most significant outcomes from the work of this committee was the widespread adoption of the Carnegie unit that led to formulas for credit transfer. In 1918, a Committee of Nine on the Articulation of High School and College reaffirmed college preparation as a high school responsibility.

The most important of the early national agencies created to study higher education was the Truman Commission. Published by the Commission in 1947, *Higher Education for American Democracy* gave immediate attention to the two-year college, recommending expansion of the institution as an extension of high school. These junior colleges would offer the first half of the baccalaureate degree, as well as terminal, semiprofessional courses and public service for all citizens. This prestigious report gave immediate impetus to articulation and transfer.

1950s and 1960s

The Truman Commission report set the stage for increased efforts to establish the junior college as a legitimate academic institution. The Servicemen's Readjustment Act of 1944 created an explosion of activities affecting school and college relations, and encouraged program and academic flexibility through the GED testing program under the American Council on Education and the Advanced Placement Program announced in 1955 by the College Entrance Examination Board.

The Fifty-fifth Yearbook of the National Society for the Study of Education, *The Public Junior College* (1956), was the first of several landmark publications. Bird's chapter in this volume, "Preparation for Advanced Study," described the magnitude of the transfer function. After examining scores of transfer success studies, Bird concluded that "junior college transfers make records approximately the same as those made by transfers from four-year colleges and by native students, sometimes excelling slightly and sometimes being slightly excelled by the other groups. They usually show a drop in their grade average in the first term after transfer but then recover that loss" (p. 85). She also referred to evidence that junior colleges were salvaging many students who otherwise would not have opportunities for advanced studies. Because of these observations, she called for mutual understanding and cooperation in determining transfer policies.

A year later, a national committee was created by the Association of American Colleges and the American Association of Junior Colleges. The following year, 1958, the American Association of Collegiate Registrars and Admissions Officers, headed by Clyde Vroman, joined the two associations to form the Joint Committee on Junior and Senior Colleges. Under the chairmanship of James Wattenbarger, the joint committee created a set of transfer guidelines. In 1959, the Joint Committee requested the University of California, Berkeley Center for the Study of Higher Education to develop studies on characteristics and transfer problems of junior college graduates. Two studies were carried out that focused on these areas and resulted in two technical reports by Knoell and Medsker, published by the Center in 1963–64. A reader's version, *From Junior to Senior College,* was published in 1965. The research methodology used in the Knoell and Medsker studies remains a standard for future investigations of those seeking to measure progress toward equal opportunity. This effort, involving some forty-three colleges in ten states, ranks with Koos's work some forty years earlier as the most significant research conducted on the articulation and transfer phenomenon. Also, Medsker's book *The Junior College: Progress and Prospect* (1960) carries extensive references to transfer student performance, retention, and problems, as well as faculty attitudes. This landmark contribution is the only early book on the two-year college to make more than cursory reference to articulation as here defined.

Early state master plans lacked information on articulation and transfer. However, the Master Plan for Higher Education in California 1968–1975, establishing a tripartite system in that state, recommended policies and procedures for intersegmental transfer. The need to improve articulation services, counseling in particular, was also strongly documented in the California Master Plan, but implementation continued on a volunteer basis, not as a state government responsibility. During the 1960s, similar intersegmental volunteer efforts were also developing in Illinois, Michigan, and Washington under the initiative of the major universities in those states. Developments in four states presaged greater state government attention to articulation and transfer: Florida (1965–66), Illinois (same year), Georgia (1969), and Texas (same year). (See Kintzer, 1976 for details of these and other developments.)

1970s

The 1970s were a period of proliferation for community college transfer and articulation research. By the end of the decade, college enrollments—which had risen due to widespread financial aid programs like the GI Bill—would level off at about three in eight people attending college, up from one in seven in the mid-twentieth century (Cohen and Brawer, 1989). The growth in funding and student populations was matched by a growth in the interest of researchers, and the literature of this decade provides a fairly clear picture of the status of articulation and transfer in the community colleges for this era.

A Nationwide Pilot Study on Articulation (Kintzer, 1970) was the first in a series of publications in this time frame devoted to articulation and transfer. The objective of this topical paper was to present summaries of articulation and transfer policies and procedures in the fifty states. A preliminary typology of state styles was also offered, updated, and expanded in later publications.

College Transfer (Association Transfer Group, 1974), a compilation of six papers of the Airlie House Conference on College Transfer in Virginia, highlighted the first half of the decade. At this conference the Association Transfer Group (ATG), convened by the American Council on Education, responded to recommendations of the Commission on Non-Traditional Study concerning the attempts of nontraditional or unconventional students to move through systems of higher education. The six Airlie House papers were the major contributions of the early 1970s. Diversity and breadth characterized the recommendations. Separate sets of suggestions were directed to faculties, institutional administrators, accrediting agencies and state agencies, legislators and federal executive agencies, and national organizations.

Professional association and research conference discussions were primarily concerned with policies and methods to assist itinerant students in entering and reentering higher education systems. The primacy of institutions was emphasized, and so-called third parties, beyond unilateral institutional efforts, were urged to assist. These included regional, state, national, and international agencies. Probably for the first time in a national forum, the entry and reentry of various transfer types were given serious and exhaustive consideration.

Another strategic publication of the 1970s is Kintzer's *Middleman in Higher Education* (1973). Part Two, "The Articulation Scene," outlines statewide patterns and summarizes policies in the fifty states. *Understanding Diverse Students* (Knoell, 1973), a product of the continuing series New Directions for Community Colleges, is another significant publication in this time period. The focus of this monograph is "the education and guidance of students from widely varying backgrounds and with diverse interests and objectives" (p. vii).

Menacker (1975) was the first to deal explicitly with problems of horizontal articulation: for example, curricular integration; general education within a level of schooling; guidance-centered articulation as the focus of vertical articulation; atypical needs of minority students; and other topics theretofore mentioned by authors, but unexplored.

Credentialing Educational Accomplishment (1978), edited by Miller and Mills, climaxed a two-year study by an American Council on Education (ACE) task force. This is the first book to deal comprehensively with the educational and social implications of credits, certificates, diplomas, and degrees.

The 1970s ended with the publication of "Transferring Experiential Learning," edited by Martorana and Kuhns (1979). The eleven-article volume accounts for gaps in the transfer and articulation process associated with credit for extrainstitutional or experiential learning, and the increasing portability of such credit.

1980s

Several reports of national importance and the second edition of *Guidelines for Improving Articulation Between Community/Junior and Senior Colleges* (1983), developed by the joint task force of six national associations, were significant contributions among a rapidly growing number of published studies found in the literature of the 1980s. The second edition of *Guidelines* closely follows the pattern of the initial 1967 publication. More attention is given in the second edition to problems encountered by reverse transfers, interinstitutional and intersegmental transfers, and other more recently identified groups. During this time frame, the work of Richard Richardson also signaled the developing interest in helping minorities achieve degrees.

Among the reports in this decade, "Improving Articulation and Transfer Relationships" (Kintzer, 1982) was released during a period of economic constraint, increasing pressure from state governments, and competition among senior institutions to enroll ever greater numbers of transfers. Diminishing numbers of traditional transfer age cohorts added to the restive situation. The goal of that volume was to open a new era of revitalizing articulation and transfer through dialogue among national leaders.

Following in the footsteps of the report just mentioned, *The Articulation/Transfer Phenomenon: Patterns and Directions* (Kintzer and Wattenbarger, 1985) identified a typology of four state patterns of articulation and transfer agreements, preceded by a synopsis of the transfer situation, and followed by a glimpse of formal and informal credit transfer arrangements in other countries. The four state patterns of transfer and articulation agreements are characterized as follows.

Formal and legally based guidelines and policies. Legal or quasi-legal contracts mandated by state law, state code, or a higher education master plan in which general education is recognized for transfer; includes an emphasis on completion of A.A. degree prior to transfer. These types of policies are evident in approximately eight states, of which the Florida Formal Agreement Plan and Illinois Legally-Based Plan are examples.

State system policies. Guidelines that concentrate more on the transfer process and less on articulation services; there is stronger and more direct state control. This pattern occurs in approximately twenty-five states; examples are New Jersey's Full-Faith-and-Credit Policy and the Oklahoma State System Plan.

Voluntary agreements among institutions. Informal processes or voluntary cooperation and negotiation for which discussions often surround subject matter and concern intersegmental liaison committees. Approximately twenty-eight states follow this pattern; the Washington Intercollege Relations Commission and the California Intersegmental Articulation Committee Action are examples.

Special agreements on vocational and technical credit transfer. Arrangements made within a few states to accept designated vocational and technical course credit. Examples are the Michigan Mandated Policies and the North Carolina Health Articulation Project.

Finally, Cohen and Brawer's book, *The Collegiate Function of Community Colleges* (1987) is an important contribution to the literature that should be mentioned to complete the decade. This text is a comprehensive examination of articulation and transfer primarily from a liberal arts education perspective.

Leading into the 1990s

Several themes in articulation and transfer appearing in the 1980s literature gained major recognition in the first half of the 1990s and merit some attention here.

Access to Higher Education for Disadvantaged Populations. The first theme concerns efforts to improve the scope and individual numbers of disadvantaged groups with an emphasis on ethnic minorities. The Ford Foundation-sponsored Urban Community College Transfer Opportunity Program (UCC/TOP) led the upsurge of activities in this area. Donovan and Associates' (1987) work *Transfer: Making It Work* offered innovative examples of programs to confirm that progress in increasing minority access could be seen best by taking a look at individual colleges. State support, in general, continues to lag for increasing minority involvement and for improving programmatic quality. However, progress is still occurring in individual colleges and groups of collaborating schools with considerable help from private funding agencies.

Vocational-Technical Education. Several decades ago, virtually the only transfer avenue for vocational-technical credits was the university baccalaureate degree. Programmatic diversification and flexible delivery schedules implemented to compensate for static academic enrollments and budgets in both two- and four-year colleges attracted career-oriented high school graduates, and other potential graduates. Dale Parnell, the most visible single personality in promoting cooperative vocational and technical programs, gave national recognition to the 2+2 tech-prep/associate degree format in his 1985 book *The Neglected Majority.* In *Dateline 2000: The New Higher Education Agenda* (1990), Parnell continues his advocacy of vocational and technical education but introduces new themes under the goal of serving at-risk populations.

Also, in *Enhancing Articulation and Transfer,* Prager (1988) accounts for the intervention of private foundations, state legislation, and interstate commissions, and gives particular attention to improving community college academic studies. In the final chapter of this topical volume, Prager focuses on transfer options for occupational-technical majors. She refers to a "climate of negativity" surrounding the limited literature of community college vocationalism (p. 79).

Business and Industry, the Military, and Proprietary Schools. Employer-sponsored education, proprietary school training, and training for the military provided externally by colleges and universities are forces severely affecting articulation and transfer that emerged in the 1970s and gathered strength in the 1980s. As the first two "outsiders" were granted accreditation by regional agencies and began to form legitimate linkages with state and private institutions, the need for guidelines and policies became crucial. Relationships between proprietary schools and their counterparts in public education—community colleges—remain strained. Some attempt to work together and to exchange students can be traced to individual institutions, but again, transfer agreements are virtually nonexistent. Several states have developed such statements, but the courses, degree programs, and students wanting to transfer remain virtually unrecognized.

Computerized Information Systems. Colleges and universities are still criticized for collecting and distributing invalid and unreliable student data, transfer data in particular. This chaotic situation confuses state commissions, whose reports to state legislatures are often inaccurate and inconsistent. Although all institutions and systems collect relevant information, few have databases that provide current transfer information on students, counselors, and faculty, or reliable information on student tracking. The lack of common definition and consistent reporting complicates the budgetary process and weakens attempts to develop statewide policy.

1990s

The themes emerging from the 1980s are reflected in the literature of the 1990s. The final decade of the century opened auspiciously with an announcement by the American Association of Community and Junior Colleges (AACJC) Board of Directors declaring that 1990 would be the Year of the Transfer. Two publications are primary references reflecting the issues of the decade: *Transfer, Articulation, Collaboration: Twenty-Five Years Later,* by Knoell (1990), and Bender's *Spotlight on the Transfer Function: National Study of State Policies and Practices* (1990).

The research directed by Knoell (1990) reexamines the 1961–64 Knoell-Medsker study. The two efforts, twenty-five years apart, were actually quite different. The second focused on state rather than institutional practices, and on institutional rather than student data. In the statement of general principles, a distinction is made between transfer and articulation, in part to accommodate the greatly increased complexity of the process of exchanging students and credits. Transfer is recognized "as the process of aligning courses and programs that are offered by two or more institutions" (p. 78).

The second major work of the 1990s, *Spotlight on the Transfer Function* (Bender, 1990), consists of seven papers covering state-level policies, including a model of state-level articulation information, and case reports of successful transfer and articulation in four states. In Part One, an idealized model of state-level articulation information systems is described by Odum. Part Two offers a series of case studies in three states where universities are collaborating with community colleges—New Jersey, Florida, and California.

Other projects in the 1990s have also contributed to improving transfer and articulation. Community college centers at George Mason and UCLA were major contributors to a two-year college transfer project to define methodology for calculating transfer rates. NCAAT personnel were responsible for reporting various transfer strategies among two- and four-year institutions, how transfer students were identified, and how transfer rates were established. The George Mason Center for Community College Education gathered information on processes involved in obtaining transfer numbers and determining the validity of such calculations. The UCLA Center for the Study of Community Colleges concentrated on defining and calculating a common transfer rate for all two-year colleges. In a 1994 monograph, Cohen presents a convincing case for the indispensable need for data collected uniformly across the states. One additional work worthy of note is Eaton's (1994) *Strengthening the Collegiate Education in Community Colleges.* In this work she summarizes and synthesizes the theoretical perspectives of the purposes and goals of community colleges. In doing so, she builds a case for returning the collegiate function to a dominant role in the community college mission. She stresses college-level competencies as a key commitment. Her definition of the collegiate function incorporates a commitment to applied fields or career education, in addition to the liberal arts. The college-level criterion should, in her judgment, be applied to both academic and career (occupational) education. Her work touches on the heart of the controversy over the collegiate function in the 1990s.

Historical Trends Shaping Articulation and Transfer

Under several time frames, I have accounted for the major developments throughout the ninety-year history of published material on articulation and transfer, describing the transitions from simple transfer arrangements, often dictated by universities, to complex documents involving many types of transfer applicants and a wide variety of educational and noneducational organizations.

The following statements serve two purposes: to summarize changes in the articulation and transfer phenomenon as shown by the literature, and to suggest trends.

State legislatures, through commissions and agencies of government, are endorsing, even mandating, policies and procedures to control articulation and transfer. Public institutions are pressured for greater prescription.

State governments are continuing to mandate assessment procedures as bases for first admission of transfers and advance credit.

Demand is mounting for fixed formulas for reporting transfer numbers that are indicators of student success. Although the need for regularizing data is widely accepted, the wisdom of a fixed formula and the acceptance of announced equations remains under heavy debate.

Equal access for underrepresented groups continues to be a priority of community colleges.

Strengthening associate degrees has also become a national priority, as responsibility for remediation has shifted in practice from universities to community colleges.

Relations between high schools and community colleges are expanding through two-two programs, and extending into universities through two-two-two arrangements.

Greater attention is being given to services for transfer students in statewide formulas and individual agreements.

Informal transfer alliances with employer-sponsored institutes are rapidly developing, but formal alliances, for example, integrated degree programs and other cooperative efforts, are emerging more slowly.
Except in islands of activity, proprietary school and community college collaboration remains virtually unattended.
Policies on credit transfer for experiential (prior) learning are appearing, as well as formal schooling for the military and various types of continuing education.

A closing thought from Richard Millard is directed to policy makers and practitioners who wish to improve articulation and transfer. "Given student mobility and the range of postsecondary opportunities available, transfer of credit should be based not on formal institutional peer-group equivalence but on substantive knowledge and competency attained and should be assessed in the light of student and . . . institutional objectives in the program into which the student is transferring" (Millard, 1991, p. 65). Need we be reminded that a college education is no longer just a privilege? As viewed by the millions across the land and around the world, it is a right not to be denied.

References

American Council on Education. *Guidelines for Improving Articulation Between Community/Junior and Senior Colleges.* Washington, D.C.: American Council on Education, 1983.

Association Transfer Group. *College Transfer: Working Papers and Recommendations from the Airlie House Conference 2–4. December 1973.* Washington, D.C.: American Council on Higher Education, 1974.

Bender, L. W. *Spotlight on the Transfer Function: A National Study of State Policy.* Washington, D.C.: American Association of Community and Junior Colleges, 1990. (ED 317 246)

Bird, G. V. "Preparation for Advanced Study." *The Public Junior College.* Chicago: Fifty-fifth Yearbook of the National Society for the Study of Education, 1956.

Cohen, A. M. (ed.). *Relating Curriculum and Transfer.* New Directions for Community Colleges, no. 86. San Francisco: Jossey-Bass, 1994.

Cohen, A. M., and Brawer, F. B. *The Collegiate Function of Community Colleges.* San Francisco: Jossey-Bass, 1987.

Cohen, A. M., and Brawer, F. B. *The American Community College.* (2nd ed.) San Francisco: Jossey-Bass, 1989.

Donovan, R. A. (ed.). *Transfer: Making It Work.* Washington, D.C.: American Association of Community and Junior Colleges, 1987. (ED 281 579)

Eaton, J. S. *Strengthening Collegiate Education in Community Colleges.* San Francisco: Jossey-Bass, 1994.

Eells, W. C. *The Junior College.* New York: Houghton Mifflin, 1931.

Kintzer, F. C. *Nationwide Pilot Study on Articulation.* Topical Paper no. 15. Los Angeles: ERIC Clearinghouse for Junior Colleges, 1970. (ED 045 065)

Kintzer, F. C. *The Middleman in Higher Education.* San Francisco: Jossey-Bass, 1973.

Kintzer, F. C. *Articulation and Transfer.* Topical Paper no. 59. Los Angeles: ERIC Clearinghouse for Junior Colleges, 1976. (ED 130 746)

Kintzer, F. C. *Improving Articulation and Transfer Relationships.* New Directions for Community Colleges, no. 39. San Francisco: Jossey-Bass, 1982.

Kintzer, F. C., and Wattenbarger, J. L. *The Articulation/Transfer Phenomenon: Patterns and Directions.* Washington, D.C.: American Association of Community and Junior Colleges, 1985.

Knoell, D. M. (ed.). *Understanding Diverse Students*. New Directions for Community Colleges, no. 3. San Francisco: Jossey-Bass, 1973.

Knoell, D. M. *Transfer, Articulation, Collaboration: Twenty-Five Years Later*. Washington, D.C.: American Association of Community and Junior Colleges, 1990. (ED 318 528)

Knoell, D. M., and Medsker, L. L. *From Junior to Senior College: A National Study of the Transfer Student*. Washington, D.C.: American Council on Education, 1965. (ED 013 632)

Koos, L. V. *The Junior College*. 3 vols. Minneapolis, Minn.: University of Minnesota Press, 1924.

Koos, L. V. *Integrating High School and College: The Six-Four-Four Plan at Work*. New York: Harper, 1946.

Liaison Committee of the State Board of Education and the Regents of the University of California. *A Master Plan For Higher Education in California*. (1968–1975). Sacramento: California State Department of Education, 1968.

Martorana, S. V., and Kuhns, E. (eds.). *Transferring Experiential Learning*. New Directions for Experiential Learning, no.4. San Francisco: Jossey-Bass, 1979.

McDowell, F. M. *The Junior College. Bulletin No. 35*. Washington, D.C.: U.S. Bureau of Education, 1919.

Medsker, L. L. *The Junior College: Progress and Prospect*. New York: McGraw-Hill, 1960.

Menacker, J. *From School To College: Articulation and Transfer*. Washington, D.C.: American Council on Education, 1975.

Millard, R. M. *Today's Myths and Tomorrow's Realities*. San Francisco: Jossey-Bass, 1991.

Miller, J. W., and Mills, O. (eds.). *Credentialing Educational Accomplishment*. Washington, D.C.: American Council on Education, 1978.

Parnell, D. *The Neglected Majority*. Washington, D.C.: Community College Press, 1985.

Parnell, D. *Dateline 2000: The New Higher Education Agenda*. Washington, D.C.: Community College Press, 1990.

Prager, C. (ed.). *Enhancing Articulation and Transfer*. New Directions for Community Colleges, no. 61. San Francisco: Jossey-Bass, 1988.

President's Commission on Higher Education. *Higher Education for American Democracy*. 6 vols. New York: Harper, 1947.

Richardson, R. C., Fisk, E. C., and Okum, M. A. *Literacy in the Open-Access College*. San Francisco: Jossey-Bass, 1983. (ED 320 650)

Witt, A., Wattenbarger, J. L., Gollattscheck, J. F., and Suppiger, J. E. *America's Community Colleges: The First Century*. Washington, D.C.: American Association of Community Colleges, 1994. (ED 368 415)

Frederick C. Kintzer is professor emeritus at the Graduate School of Education and Information Studies, University of California, Los Angeles, and national lecturer, Nova Southeastern University, Ft. Lauderdale, Florida.

In order to ensure that higher education institutions provide the most education for the money they are allocated, it is important for states to determine policy to encourage cooperation and reduce redundancy in educational missions.

The Role of the State in Transfer and Articulation

Piedad F. Robertson, Ted Frier

The question is not whether states will be more aggressive in promoting transfer and articulation in higher education, but how soon, and how much, in what form, and for whom. Greater state involvement is a given. The impacts on limited state budgets, the implications for the economic stability and competitiveness of the states, and the obligations of states to their citizens to guarantee educational opportunities are simply too urgent to delegate this responsibility to the ad hoc, accidental, voluntary arrangements that colleges may or may not entertain depending on their own peculiar interests or circumstances.

The New Environment

Twenty-five years ago there was almost no state involvement in transfer and articulation. Today, according to a Ford Foundation survey, all fifty states have some form of higher education coordinating authority, and most are actively involved in promoting integrated programs between the education segments and their institutions (Knoell, 1990). Many states have enunciated formal and precise articulation agreements. Some have established state agencies with statutory powers to direct transfer activities. Many fund specialized services for transfer students. Others require colleges to collect and report performance data on transfer students. In some states transfer remains voluntary. Others make it mandatory.

Oregon, as an example, requires its State Board of Higher Education to work with the State Board of Education to ensure that students passing an associate of arts program at community colleges meet the lower-division general education requirements of four-year public institutions. Florida established a state Articulation Coordinating Committee to ensure that students with an associate in arts degree are guaranteed admission to and credit at the state's baccalaureate institutions. The Articulation Council of California acts as a liaison to the state's higher education institutions to develop guidelines on program articulation (Knoell, 1990). These are just a few examples that illustrate that when asked to choose between formalized coordination and traditional prerogatives of autonomy, states are siding with coordination. This new interest in transfer and articulation issues is not an isolated idiosyncracy on the part of states. The expansion of transfer and articulation agreements is occurring today as a natural and predictable consequence of efforts by various states to reform and reorganize their education systems to meet the multiple demands of educating a vastly larger and more diverse population for a highly complex economy in a time of limited financial resources.

The world that students are entering is radically different from that of a generation ago. Today, the most industrious worker must have many of the same skills once possessed only by well-trained professionals. Therefore, there has been a growing urgency for public education systems to do better. Once attention to public education reached critical mass, it emerged as a political priority, pressuring public officials at all levels—local, state, and federal—to do something to improve the schools.

Almost without exception, individual states have responded with comprehensive legislation to improve their primary and secondary education systems. The best of these laws delegate much more authority to the local level—the parents, teachers, and principals at the individual schools. Yet there is no question that these reform measures define a larger role for the state in local public education than in the past. The commonality between these seemingly contradictory initiatives is the underlying conviction of policy makers that the key to improving the quality of education lies in new arrangements that unite the involvement and resources of the entire community, and each segment of the education system. From kindergarten and high school through higher education, public school systems are being reconfigured so that they truly function as a unified system.

These principles of collaboration, coordination, and cooperation contained in the education reform initiatives spearheaded by the states are also the principles that support transfer and articulation agreements in higher education. States are developing transfer and articulation arrangements not because they are attractive benefit programs that save students time, money, and aggravation, but because they embody the same principles that states are employing to improve the educational system. A course of study formulated with the joint involvement of high schools, community colleges, and four-year institutions will have a clearer vision of goals, a more thoughtful inventory of student competencies, and a greater likelihood of success than any college curriculum created without the benefit of this collaboration. A student's progress through the segments of the education system will have a greater likelihood of success when transfer requirements are firmly established.

The New State Commitment

As Bender, among others, has noted, the 1980s was a decade when responsibility for transfer and articulation in public higher education shifted from the local level to the state. Through state policy and the budget process, there is an identifiable shift of authority in the area of student transfer from departmental faculties to state-level bodies and agencies. Certain colleges and universities have a history of supporting transfer and articulation, and state action is not superseding those efforts. However, the failure on the part of all colleges and universities to work closely together on transfer education and corresponding articulation agreements has created a vacuum that is being filled by state mandates (Bender, 1990).

According to Bender, "[a]ttitudes on higher education have changed in the last few decades as higher education is seen as more of a right as well as a requirement for competing globally. The key players have moved from admissions officers in the 1960s, to transfer/articulation officers in the 1980s, to faculty groups in the 1990s as states begin to take transfer and articulation seriously. There is a perception in many states that students are being treated unfairly when transferring from one institution to another. The general public and their elected representatives perceive publicly sponsored or supported postsecondary institutions as a system of interdependent and complementary elements that fit together as a whole, not as different, competing elements. Education is viewed as a process, not institutional forms or types" (p. 6).

In 1989 alone, thirteen states passed new laws on transfer and articulation. These were prescriptive mandates for the higher education system. The accumulation of so many new laws on transfer by so many states in such a brief span of time had the effect of "communicating to faculties an intolerance of perceived abuses to the interest of the student and the taxpayer" (p. 5).

There are a number of reasons for this bustle of state activity. First, states are better organized than they once were. When the Ford Foundation first did a survey of transfer activity in 1965, it found, not surprisingly, little in the way of comprehensive, statewide policy in the area of higher education. Few states even had a central higher education agency when that survey was taken. Following passage of the federal Higher Education Act of 1972, central coordinating agencies were created in virtually all fifty states, and part of their responsibility has been to coordinate student transfer and program articulation (Knoell, 1990).

Second, the demands on higher education to produce graduates prepared to meet the demands of a complex and competitive economy have grown massively. Third, because of these new demands on the states' education systems, the states themselves have grown more accustomed to taking an active role in education. The number of states that have passed, or are in the process of pass-ing, major reform laws to overhaul their education systems attests to that. Most states are predisposed to leave the details of how the product is delivered to the professionals at the local school level, but they reserve the right to deter-mine what is delivered.

Fourth, demographic changes are forecasting that a growing percentage of the future workforce, in most states, will be immigrants and minorities. Many of these workers will need a college education if states are to remain compet-itive, and it is precisely these workers who typically begin their college careers in a community or junior college. Additionally, the changes in the economy have created a whole new class of workers who are pursuing, or will need to pursue, a college degree. These students are nontraditional according to the categories still in use, but they are not uncommon. The nature of today's econ-omy requires that workers change jobs, and often careers, half a dozen times over the course of their lifetimes. The ongoing transition from heavy manu-facturing to a service and information economy has resulted in a substantial new market of students for colleges and universities. Many of these new stu-dents are older workers, with family commitments, who have no postsec-ondary education. These are students one would expect to reenter the education system at a local community college, perhaps repeatedly, as their careers change.

Finally, the budgetary constraints that all states must contend with are a factor in increased state involvement. Forced to stretch their dollars, states are not prepared to see them wasted in student aid or college appropriations, when better coordination between public institutions can produce the same results for less.

Distilling the experiences of the states, national educational organizations like the American Council on Education and the American Association of Community and Junior Colleges have offered guidelines in the following three areas to help the states navigate these unfamiliar shoals.

Policy directions. Governors and state legislatures should give broad pol-icy direction on transfer and articulation, and provide general oversight, but refrain from mandating admissions standards and transferability of courses. The governing boards for systems of two- and four-year institutions should adopt policies and regulations that implement state policy and review infor-mation being sent to state coordinating agencies for problems in student flow and articulation that need attention.

Special programs and services. Governors and legislatures should develop special programs and services to support transfer and articulation, and should provide funding for such projects on a pilot basis. Admission with advanced standing should not be restricted to applicants who have completed an asso-ciate of arts degree, but instead should be open to any applicant who has com-pleted an appropriate lower-division program for transfer.

Dissemination of transfer information. The guidelines suggest that states should develop systems to ensure that students are informed about transfer

opportunities. States should use financial support to aid students who transfer. They should establish benchmarks to measure transfer success, and hold
institutions accountable for transfer success. In addition, states should expand
efforts to build academic relationships between faculty and departments at
two- and four-year institutions (Knoell, 1990).

The thrust of these recommendations, as Knoell has said, is "toward uni-
formity and simplicity to insure the fair and equal treatment of all transfer students by all four-year institutions. A major objective is to motivate students to
continue their education to develop their full potential by allowing them to
keep their options open and move from level to level with as little loss of time
and duplication of effort as possible" (p. 79).

Arenas of State Involvement. The involvement of states in transfer and
articulation manifests itself in a number of arenas. It can be seen in the creation of specialized governance structures to coordinate transfer and articulation activities. It is evident in the use of student aid and state budget allocations
to higher education institutions to drive transfer activities and college missions.
State interest is apparent in the development of uniform course numbering systems to define course equivalencies that promote transfer opportunities. It can
be seen in state efforts to create technology networks in education that are necessary to support the administrative procedures that direct a comprehensive
transfer system. State involvement is also apparent in the development of
coherent and distinctive admission standards that help define differences
between the sectors of higher education, refine institutional mission, and thus
direct the flow of students to and between the institutional sectors.

Governance Structures. Any attempt by the states to impose a system
on public higher education risks a formidable confrontation with history. Governance in higher education is more honored in theory than in practice. Individual institutions, and especially faculties and departments within those
institutions, are accustomed to uncommon autonomy in comparison to other
public service agencies. Autonomy, and the delegation of admission and curricular decisions to departments and faculty, were two factors cited by Knoell
as mitigating against enforceable statewide transfer policies (1990).

As a result, whatever transfer and articulation agreements did exist in the
past were the products of institutions rather than states. In some states the
record was exemplary. Whether it involved individual department faculty in
selected disciplines, four-year institutions and their feeder schools, or groups
of institutions, voluntary transfer and articulation agreements were arranged.

California, North Carolina, South Carolina, and Illinois were cited in the
Ford Foundation report as offering examples of productive voluntary transfer
and articulation activities that progressed without legislative involvement. For
more than sixty-five years, the Articulation Council of California brought the
various systems and segments of the state higher education system together to
develop guidelines on articulation. The Joint Committee on College Transfer Students in North Carolina is a voluntary twelve-member committee appointed by
the University of North Carolina, the State Department of Community Colleges,

and the Association of Independent Colleges and Universities. It publishes guidelines for transfer. The South Carolina Commission on Higher Education has brought together the state's four-year and two-year institutions to develop transfer credit for students who complete the associate in arts or associate in science degrees. The Articulation Compact of Illinois was reached through a voluntary agreement between the state's four- and two-year institutions. More common than even these voluntary statewide plans were the agreements reached by individual institutions and department faculties (California Postsecondary Education Commission, 1990).

But voluntary agreements alone do not meet the states' demands for greater transfer opportunities for their students. Many states are taking matters into their own hands. The Ford Foundation study cited Colorado, Florida, Illinois, Washington, and Minnesota as examples where policies on transfer and articulation have been mandated legislatively.

Among the states, Florida has perhaps gone further than most in its regulation of transfer and articulation. The Florida legislature has made direct statutory provision for student transfer, and has created a central state agency to ensure its implementation. In Illinois, the legislature directed the Board of Higher Education to adopt an admissions policy that emphasized high school preparation in academic subjects for those entering baccalaureate programs directly, or for first-time students attending a community college who hope to transfer later. Washington State recently created a Higher Education Coordinating Board and gave it responsibility to direct student transfer and articulation. Minnesota grants its Coordinating Board for Higher Education the statutory authority to monitor credit transferability, but leaves the actual development of articulation agreements to the state's community colleges and two state universities.

Technology. A common dilemma endemic to all states taking more responsibility for transfer and articulation, as Odom has said, is that there is "centralized decision making without centralized information" (1990, p. 23). However, recent investment in educational technology to physically link schools at all levels permits a range of activities that support articulated programs. Student transcripts can be instantaneously exchanged, a single college application is possible, and matching course definitions with uniform standards and prerequisites can be developed for the entire higher education system. Technology permits guidance counselors at community colleges to better advise their students with up-to-date information on what courses can be transferred. Investment in technology has an additional benefit—it enhances accountability, as higher education officials are able to give high schools reports on student performance, and universities can report to community colleges on the performance of transfer students in a similar manner.

Several states have even developed computerized academic advisement systems to aid in guidance. Florida's Student On-Line Advisement and Registration system (SOLAR) provides community college students with an academic plan according to their selected major and upper-division institution. California appropriated funds in 1985 for the implementation of an interactive, computerized transfer information system on selected community college and university campuses known as ASSIST (Articulation System Stimulating Interinstitutional Student Transfer). This project is a joint development of a federally funded four-state articulation project of the Western Interstate Commission on Higher Education. ASSIST provides access to accurate and comprehensive information on transfer alternatives; a means of determining the transferability of courses; access to a student's individual progress toward satisfying requirements for transfer; and a way of identifying specific courses that may be taken in lieu of requirements (Knoell, 1990).

Most technological systems designed to track student progress from one educational level to another are still in their infancy. Existing databases and networks cannot yet adequately track students as they transfer between institutions and programs, nor provide these students with the information about courses and programs to help them make these transitions.

Beyond the administrative benefits of technology, linking higher education institutions also aids transfer and articulation by allowing four-year institutions to offer baccalaureate instruction to remote sites and new markets via distance learning. These technology linkages obviously enhance the educational opportunities of students already in the higher education system. But often overlooked is the role that technology can play in connecting higher education with secondary education. Technology can be a powerful tool for making higher education an active participant in K-12 education reform by allowing college faculty to assist in curricula development and teacher preparation and performance. From these interactions are sown the seeds of later program articulation arrangements.

Admissions Standards. State government can also neutralize one of the most severe impediments to transfer: competition for students. Understandably, the time to interest a college or university in expanding its transfer options is not when the institution is squeezed by a shortage of students. When enrollments are down, institutions typically react by erecting barriers against admitting transfer students, while simultaneously recruiting students who might be better served somewhere else. States can nullify much of this destructive competition for student enrollments by developing and enforcing admissions standards that accurately reflect the distinct missions of each educational segment and express the educational requirements and qualifications that institutions have for their students. The need for improved admissions requirements is clear. Many admissions policies today, says Knoell, "appear to be based more on philosophy and the marketplace than on research to improve the prediction of who is most likely to succeed" (1990, p. 64).

Without clear and consistent admissions standards, states cannot distinguish with any precision the difference between the mission of a university and that of the local community college, and, therefore, attempts to contain costs, limit program duplication, and indirectly promote transfer opportunities are pointless and futile. To enforce clear and consistent admissions standards, states are increasingly adopting a standardized assessment of basic student skills, like Florida's Rising Junior Exam. Assessment and remediation policies vary, "but they have in common the principle that students should not progress to the upper division until or unless they have shown that they are proficient in the requisite basic skills," (Knoell, 1990, p. 27).

These tests are used both as an accountability measure to maintain the distinctiveness of each higher education sector, and as a protective measure that ensures that those students who demonstrate mastery of basic skills will not be denied transfer to upper-division programs. For students whose skills are judged to be deficient, remedial programs can be recommended. To maintain the distinctiveness of the institutions in higher education, many states are also requiring that all remedial programs be offered through community colleges.

Financial Incentives. A state's ability to create effective opportunities for its citizens to transfer easily among public higher education institutions resides in the state's financial power. As the amount of state funds for public higher education becomes more limited, the states have begun taking a second look at academic programs their colleges and universities are offering and demanding that the various segments and institutions refine their educational goals and missions. In this way, states eliminate needless duplication while permitting colleges and universities to improve the quality of instruction by redirecting their resources toward more finite and manageable academic programs.

Though the imposition of a more streamlined approach to higher education programs may have been launched for fiscal reasons, it has obvious implications for transfer and articulation. As state coordinating agencies, together with state legislatures, work to ensure that public funds are used efficiently, not wasted on duplicate programs, it becomes particularly important for states to promote a diversity of campus missions and cooperation among institutions. Although transfer and articulation may not be an absolute standard applied to a state's review of proposed or existing academic programs, researchers report that in states where transfer and articulation are identified priorities, statewide planning does include an examination of how those college programs will provide transfer opportunities.

Coordinating the mission of the public higher education system and the missions of the individual institutions within those systems has become a paramount responsibility of the states. By connecting budget appropriations to these clearly articulated and limited missions, states are able to ensure that the system functions with no unnecessary duplication in programs and services, and that these clearly defined roles promote coordination and collaboration among community colleges, state colleges, and universities.

Beyond directing institutional missions through budget appropriations, states can use other financial incentives to promote transfer and articulation. Some states provide special state funding for programs to increase or facilitate transfer and articulation. California is a good example of this. In other states, federal and private foundation grants are used, and special appropriations have been made to support transfer centers at community college and university campuses where students, faculty, student services staff, articulation officers, and others can get information or referrals about transfer and articulation. Additionally, states have expanded transfer opportunities by constructing facilities that are used jointly by two- and four-year institutions. Under Florida's Master Plan for Postsecondary Education any new public higher education construction must reflect the state's commitment to transfer and articulation.

Financial aid is another area where government can promote transfer opportunities. States can encourage transfer by making more financial aid available to students who transfer than to those who do not. The federal government could do the same by giving greater weight to transfer students in the formulas used to distribute SEOG, Work Study, and Perkins Act funds (Hauptman, 1992).

Course Equivalencies. Statewide governance structures, comprehensive admissions standards, distinctive missions, financial incentives, and technology are all integral to efforts by the states to expand educational opportunities for their citizens. However, the underlying premise of transfer and articulation is that a uniform value can be assigned to a specific body of knowledge, wherever and however it is acquired. Indeed, efforts to promote transfer and articulation are impossible unless common ground can be found among institutions on the value of certain curriculums and disciplines, or the definitions of student competencies. From their central position in the higher education system, states are particularly well placed to promote this dialogue, with carrots if possible, with sticks if necessary.

The efforts by states to assign a commonly accepted value to the education any particular student has received manifests itself in two ways: the creation of a common course numbering system to define academic equivalencies, and the designation of a common core of general education that can be acquired in a variety of settings and accepted at all public baccalaureate-degree-granting institutions. Many states have undertaken a thorough inventory of their higher education programs, whether voluntarily or spurred on by legislative mandates. Whether states have undertaken one or both of these efforts, the key to success has been the degree of faculty participation, both for the expertise they provide during the program's creation, and its later acceptance by faculty and departments once it is created.

Conclusion

The steps undertaken by state governments to improve the transfer opportunities of students are as varied as the states themselves. No single model has been pursued by all states. What all states do share in common are the goals that can only be reached through improved transfer and articulation agreements in their public higher education systems: direct budget savings for the state and its citizens; reductions in academic program duplication; improved quality of academic programs through opportunities for greater specialization; enhanced opportunities for students to pursue higher education; and, most important, the strengthened economic competitiveness of those states able to deliver a more highly educated and highly skilled workforce. As surveys reveal, all states are pursuing improvements in transfer opportunities to one degree or another. At one end of the spectrum are those states that have enacted laws compelling their public higher education institutions to work more closely together and have defined the areas in which that collaboration will occur. At the other end are those states that have used their offices to facilitate voluntary agreements between the institutions themselves. In whatever form they take, transfer and articulation in public colleges and universities are currently, and will continue to remain in the foreseeable future, a top priority of state higher education policy.

References

Bender, L. W. (ed.). *Spotlight on the Transfer Function: A National Study of State Policies and Practices.* Washington, D.C.: American Association of Community and Junior Colleges, 1990. (ED 317 246)

California Postsecondary Education Commission. *Update on Transfer, Articulation, and Collaboration: California in the Larger Picture.* Sacramento, Calif.: California Postsecondary Education Commission, June 1990.

Hauptman, A. M. *Using Financial Incentives to Improve Transfer between Two- and Four-Year Colleges.* Washington, D.C.: National Center for Academic Achievement and Transfer, Working Papers Vol. 3, no. 5, Summer 1992. (ED 346 893)

Knoell, D. *Transfer, Articulation, and Collaboration: 25 Years Later.* Washington, D.C.: American Association of Community and Junior Colleges, 1990. (ED 318 528)

Odom, W. R. "Articulation and State-Level Information Systems: A Necessary Marriage." In Bender, L. (ed.), *Spotlight on the Transfer Function: A National Study of State Policies and Practices.* Washington, D.C.: American Association of Community and Junior Colleges, 1990. (ED 317 246)

PIEDAD F. ROBERTSON *is president and superintendent of Santa Monica College and former Secretary of Education for Massachusetts.*

TED FRIER *is special assistant to the Massachusetts Commissioner of Education.*

This chapter examines the ways in which community college policy makers at all levels can come to understand the diversity of statistical information available to them. It suggests that all information must be contextualized at the local, institutional level.

Orderly Thinking About a Chaotic System

Arthur M. Cohen

The American compulsory education system is rationally organized. The students must attend, and they progress annually from one grade to the next. Courses and curriculum are designed to follow predictable paths. The faculty are monitored; the textbooks are uniform.

Higher education, in contrast, is disorderly. It is organized in a variety of forms: residential, commuter, and distance-learning institutions. The colleges award numerous degrees: associate's, bachelor's, master's, and doctorates. They are financed and governed through a variety of overlapping arrangements: public, private, and profit-making. They emphasize research, technical studies, liberal arts, and various combinations thereof.

The students in American higher education are diverse, and they cannot be categorized easily. They often end up in postsecondary education at their own convenience, stopping in and out as their life circumstances dictate. Some begin immediately upon graduating from high school, others delay entry for a decade or more. Many start in community colleges and transfer to universities, some start at universities and transfer to community colleges, and yet others begin at both types of institutions simultaneously. In addition, they attend in sporadic fashion and switch programs repeatedly. Eventually most of the students attain a certificate indicating that they have accumulated a certain number of credit hours and satisfied the requirements at some degree-granting institution.

The curriculum in American higher education is confused. It encompasses literacy studies, general education, core requirements, and electives. It centers on the liberal arts, occupational studies, and studies for an individual's personal interest. The content of what are ostensibly the same courses varies across institutions and often varies within different sections of the same course in the same institution. Some of the curriculum rests on a canon that is centuries old; other parts of it are reformed and revised continually.

Instruction is chaotic. Students may be confronted with a multimedia laboratory in their first course in a subject area whereas the succeeding course is taught through a lecture method. One class encourages students to cooperate with each other on learning projects; in another class students are expected to compete. Often the students are faced with different types of tasks within the same curriculum. They go through years of courses in which they are told what papers to write and what tests to take and then in graduate school they face independent learning situations.

Wouldn't it be easier if higher education were orderly? If institutions had distinct roles? If curriculum were composed of discrete courses, each beginning where the other ended, each with measurable entry and exit criteria? If students enrolled in the programs for which they were best suited and from which they could derive the most benefit?

But this is not the case, and because of the complexities of the higher education system an entire stratum of middle managers has arisen. Counselors, articulation officers, interinstitutional representatives, instructional coordinators, orientation-program managers, registrars and admissions practitioners, and public relations officials all attempt to bring order to the continually reforming enterprise. This chapter on student transfer from community colleges to senior institutions is addressed to them.

Access and Community Colleges

All higher education matriculants enter somewhere. The first entry is a one-time event. And it is usually a local event. In the early 1990s, less than 10 percent of the first-year students in a number of states left their home states to attend college. The states in which this occurred included Arizona, California, Michigan, Mississippi, North Carolina, Texas, and Washington, all distinguished by their having well-developed community colleges within easy commuting distance of practically everyone in the state. The states in which more than 30 percent of the first-year students left home included Connecticut, Maine, New Hampshire, New Jersey, and Vermont—states with poorly developed comprehensive community college systems (NCES, 1995). These percentages show that access and community colleges are solidly welded.

Another way of looking at the community colleges' importance in sustaining access is to compare community college enrollment with the state's population. In eighteen states the proportion of community college enrollment that is composed of African American students exceeds the proportion of African Americans in those states' populations. A similar pattern holds for Hispanics in *forty-one* states. Arizona, for example, has a population that is 9 percent Hispanic, yet 15 percent of the students in the Arizona community colleges are Hispanic. Comparable figures for California: 12 percent of the population is Hispanic and 18 percent of the students are Hispanic; in Florida, 10 and 13 percent; Colorado, 8 and 12 percent; Texas, 15 and 23 percent; and Illinois, 4 and 10 percent (Cohen and Brawer, 1996). Clearly, Hispanics are an underrepresented minority that uses the community college as its point of access to higher education.

Higher education can serve many purposes. It can prepare an individual to enter a professional career, one that otherwise denies entry to people who do not possess credentials awarded by higher education institutions. It can help people address their own interests, providing courses and programs in a variety of arenas, all leading to self improvement. It can connect people with ideas, peer groups, and institutions with which they may be proud to affiliate for a lifetime. Communities, too, take pride in their colleges, pointing to them as contributors to the economy as well as to the local culture.

Because the baccalaureate degree is the most venerable in American higher education it is often perceived as the minimum requirement to be sustained by an individual. The various attempts to have the associate's degrees and occupational certificates granted by community colleges recognized as valuable awards have borne little fruit. Many commentators contend that unless students receive the bachelor's degree they may be considered to have not completed college. The data on earnings obtained by people who have been to college show that receipt of the baccalaureate is indicative of a considerable boost in earning capacity. According to the National Center for Education Statistics, in 1992 the earnings advantage of a person with a bachelor's degree was more than double that of a person who attended only some college. For every dollar earned by a twenty-five- to thirty-four-year-old worker with twelve years of schooling, those who had from one to three years of college earned $1.17, but those with the baccalaureate or higher degrees earned $1.57 (Smith and others, 1994).

The fact that the earning capacity of people who have baccalaureate degrees is greater than that of people who do not puts the community college in a peculiar position. Half the people who begin college in America and an even higher proportion of the underrepresented minorities matriculate at community colleges. If the bachelor's degree is a requisite for major advancement, then these people must transfer to another institution if they are to be considered successful graduates. This makes transfer, only one of the community college's major missions, an essential component. Measuring transfer rates is important because it relates to the institution's passing its students through to the baccalaureate.

Transfer

Any definition for calculating transfer rates is imperfect because it excludes some pertinent data. For example, the measure must be based on some group of students: an entering set, an exiting set, or some subset within a larger group. Which group to choose? The data must be available; it is a sterile exercise to define a way of assessing the number of transfer students if the data cannot be acquired uniformly and consistently across the nation. Even though students are theoretically potential transfers until they either show up at a university or die, some finite time period must be specified in the rate calculation.

In 1989 the Center for the Study of Community Colleges set out to compute transfer rates nationwide. Determining at the outset that the definition should be valid, readily understandable, and based on data that are feasibly obtainable, the Center settled on the following formula; *all students entering the community college in a given year who have no prior college experience and who complete at least twelve college units divided into the number of that group who take one or more classes at an in-state, public university within four years.* The formula does not include student intentions, the year that the student graduated high school, students taking only academic courses, full-time students only, associate's degree recipients, or students who had completed the freshman year. It does include all students taking any type of college-credit course, including occupational courses; students who complete twelve units, which equates to one term of full-time enrollment or one course a year for four years; a four-year span between community college entrance and transfer, because few students matriculate and then move on within only a couple of years; and transfer to in-state public universities, because the independent universities in most states provide data inconsistently and data on out-of-state transfers are even more difficult to obtain.

The staff began the project by inviting samples of the nation's community colleges to participate in the Transfer Assembly. Subsequently, in 1992, the Transfer Assembly began seeking the data from the state agencies as well as from the colleges.

Soliciting the requisite information from the state higher education agencies proved considerably more fruitful. A few states have coordinated student information systems and were able to generate community college and university student information from that source; New York, Kentucky, and Colorado are examples of such states. Other states have centralized community college databases that could be matched with centralized public university databases; Illinois and North Carolina are examples of such systems. And in others there is a centralized public university student information system against which matches can be run if the data on entering students who receive twelve units can be obtained from the community colleges; Texas and California are examples of such states, the latter having two central data systems, one for the California State University system and the other for the University of California system (see Table 3.1).

By soliciting data from state agencies the number of colleges increased each year. In the fall of 1989, these colleges served as the point of first entry to higher education for 450,371 students; 228,813 of these students received at least twelve credits at the college they entered. By 1993, 48,601 of the latter had transferred to a baccalaureate-degree-granting institution. Included in the 272 colleges that provided data on their 1990 entrants were all or most of the

Table 3.1. Transfer Assembly Rate of Transfer by Year

Number of Participating Colleges	Year Students Entered	Number of Entrants	Percent Receiving 12+ Credits Within Four Years	Percent Transferring Within Four Years
48	1984	77,903	50.5	23.7
114	1985	191,748	46.7	23.6
155	1986	267,150	46.7	23.4
366	1987	507,757	46.9	22.6
395	1988	522,758	45.5	22.1
374	1989	450,371	45.1	21.2
272	1990	407,782	50.3	21.8

public community colleges in California, Colorado, Florida, Illinois, Kentucky, Louisiana, Minnesota, New Jersey, New York, North Carolina, Oklahoma, Rhode Island, Texas, and West Virginia, plus a few colleges from other states.

The year-to-year consistency in both the percent of entering students who received twelve or more credits within four years and the percent who transferred is notable, especially because the sample of colleges increased each year. Still, the national transfer rate of 21 percent masks many differences between institutions and between states. In California, for example, the overall transfer rate for the sixty-five community colleges that participated in the study was 18.1 percent, but the range was from 3 to 32 percent. Similarly, even though the transfer rate in most states with comprehensive community college systems clustered around the 22 percent national mark, individual state transfer rates ranged from 11 to 40 percent.

Minority Student Progress

The difference in high school graduation, college participation, and college graduation rates exhibited by members of various ethnic groups is reflected in the transfer-rate data. White and Asian students transfer at a rate higher than the norm, whereas African American and Hispanic students are, predictably, below the norm. These findings parallel studies of minority student progress in other sectors of higher education. As reported by the American Association of State Colleges and Universities (1994), the six-year graduation rate for white first-year students entering in 1986 was 44 percent, whereas the rate for black students was 28 percent and for Hispanics, 30 percent. Clearly, the different rates of progress are not exclusively a community college phenomenon. More-over, the national averages mask differences among individual colleges. For example, the Center study found that in colleges with transfer rates above the national norm, the African American students transferred at a rate consider-ably above their group norm and the Hispanic students transferred at a rate higher than their national norm. A comparable effect was seen in low-transfer-rate institutions; the rate for minority students dropped below the national norm for each ethnic group (Table 3.2).

Table 3.2. 1995 Transfer Assembly: Mean Transfer Percentage Rates for Students (n = 239)*

	Ethnic Groups				
	Black	Hispanic	White	Asian	Total
All colleges	12.5	12.4	23.4	23.6	21.2
Top quartile (58 colleges)	19.7	23.7	32.2	27.3	31.6
Bottom quartile (58 colleges)	6.1	5.7	9.8	9.4	8.3

*239 is the number of single colleges for which ethnic data are available. The remaining 135 colleges are not included because their transfer rates are reported as a collapsed transfer rate for particular states, districts, or state centers.

Thus, a high-transfer-rate college is a high-transfer-rate college; all groups participate when the college orientation is toward transfer. Very few students in the colleges with exceedingly low transfer rates make the move into universities, regardless of ethnicity.

Policies and Programs

Why do transfer rates vary as much as they do? Some reasons for the wide between-state disparity are obviously related to state-system structures. In states where the two-year institutions are organized as branch campuses of the state university, the transfer rates are high. In states where the colleges are organized as technical institutes that emphasize trade and industry programs, the transfer rates are low. This is not surprising; but deviations from the comprehensive-college norm appear also in states where mandates restricting college growth are imposed. Enrollment caps eventually elevate the transfer rate because the colleges tend to react by cutting the programs that attract adult, part-time students; that is, those programs that attract students who are least likely to transfer.

A few researchers have tackled the question of between-state differences. Orfield and Paul (1992) contended that in states that relied heavily on community colleges as access points, the baccalaureate attainment rate was depressed, and they concluded that the states' higher education system was at fault. Mabry (1995) found that variations in transfer rates could be predicted by whether a state's community colleges were more centered on technical than on comprehensive programs, but was unable to determine definitively that population characteristics, state structures, or state policies were influential. In states that have both comprehensive and technical colleges, Mabry's (1995) findings apply. However, in states where the colleges all ostensibly provide the same types of programs, the reasons for disparities in transfer rates must be traced to local conditions. Some conditions, such as community demographics and the college's proximity to a university campus, are immutable. Others, such as local employment or economic conditions, are beyond college control. When these powerful forces are factored out, the influence of staff-generated practices pales.

Because the within-state differences are greater than the between-state differences, the Center staff and the National Center for Academic Achievement and Transfer set up a project to investigate discernible differences between high- and low-transfer-rate colleges in the same state. College policies, history, and staff and student attitudes were assessed by interviewing college administrators and surveying a sample of students and faculty in one college selected from the highest and lowest in each of eight states. Over three thousand students on low-transfer-rate campuses and four thousand students on high-transfer-rate campuses were surveyed. In addition, 244 faculty members participated in the survey.

The findings revealed few differences between high and low colleges in a number of areas: articulation agreements; common course-numbering systems; the attitudes of faculty advisors or counselors; the presence or absence of honors programs and honors societies; the regularity of visits from university staff members; jobs for students on campus; faculty exchange between two-year and four-year institutions; mandatory orientation policies; and the types of course syllabi in use. However, a few characteristics did differentiate. High-transfer-rate colleges had a visible and vigorous transfer center staff, an accessible university with low grade-point averages for transferring students, a staff with expectations regarding transfer, and a history of high transfer even as the population of the district shifted. In addition, these campuses featured high school advanced-placement courses and a greater use of institutional research data.

The student data also revealed some differences. Students in the high-transfer-rate colleges were more likely to indicate *transfer* as their academic objective. Students from low-transfer-rate colleges more often wished to gain skills for immediate employment. Similar patterns were seen when students were asked what they considered to be the colleges' major emphases. The majority of students from high-transfer-rate colleges felt that their institutions emphasized transfer preparation; those from low-transfer-rate colleges indicated that both preparation for transfer to a four-year college and preparation for immediate employment were their colleges' primary emphases. One interesting finding was that the majority of students in both high- and low-transfer-rate colleges felt that preparation for transfer *should be* the major emphasis of their college (59 percent and 43 percent, respectively).

Despite differences in the degree to which transfer is emphasized in high- and low-transfer-rate colleges, at least 61 percent of students on both high- and low-transfer-rate campuses rated the assistance they received in the transfer process as either "somewhat or very helpful." Over 77 percent of students on both types of campuses gave similar evaluations to professors who assisted with the transfer process. In addition, students on these campuses were generous in their assessment of how their colleges affected them. Most students in both high- and low-transfer-rate colleges felt that the college "provided focus and direction," "gave [them] confidence," and "informed [them] of alternatives." Not surprisingly, students on the low-transfer-rate campuses felt their employable skills were better developed. By small margins, students on low-transfer-rate campuses also reported that the college increased their self-awareness and increased their desire for further education. More students on high-transfer-rate campuses received information about transferring to four-year colleges, whereas students on the low-transfer campuses received more information about employment opportunities. Most students on both types of campuses projected that they would be enrolled in a four-year college or university within three years of the survey.

The faculty at both low- and high-transfer-rate colleges gave similar responses when asked about their colleges' goals, emphases, and strengths. These faculty agreed that mastery and understanding, preparation for formal education, and being able to apply their skills and knowledge were the most important goals for students on their campuses. They were also most likely to indicate that being able to gain "knowledge and interest" within surrounding communities was a goal of little to no importance for their students. In addition, the faculty at both low-transfer-rate colleges and high-transfer-rate colleges believed in the importance of helping students transfer to four-year institutions. The faculty disagreed with statements that their students were "not academically qualified." As might be expected, high-transfer-rate college faculty placed somewhat more emphasis on transfer assistance than did low-transfer-rate college faculty. Faculty in both types of colleges felt that their campuses should create stronger ties with baccalaureate-degree-granting institutions. Faculty from high-transfer-rate colleges rated this as important most often.

Perhaps the faculty participating in this study invoke a realistic approach to the education of their students. Although they firmly believe in helping students attain admission to four-year colleges, they also believe in the importance of assisting students with career training and job placement. Faculty in both types of colleges stated that community colleges should emphasize developing programs to help students attain jobs after college. Understandably, more low-transfer-rate-college faculty felt this was an important emphasis—69 percent versus 48 percent in the high-transfer-rate colleges.

One hundred three administrators at these sixteen colleges were also interviewed about their colleges' policies affecting the transfer rates of their students. Their responses indicate similarities in the beliefs and perceptions of staff members at colleges with both high and low transfer rates. For example, administrators at both colleges were aware of financial aid sources available to students, and were able to describe programs such as transfer days and articulation agreements with four-year institutions.

Administrators at high-transfer campuses, however, were able to enumerate special organizational cultures and orientations that help to augment the goals and processes for transfer education. One administrator said that the "institutional mindset" of the college is the belief that they are a transfer college for their state's university system. At another college, the administrator indicated that a "general attitude of transfer prevails" on campus. Another administrator indicated that students receive institutional support for their transfer goals with the help of a college scholarship team that competes with other colleges, the assistance of counselors to help them define their own goals, and "articulation agreements signed in blood." Still another noted that upon arrival students are asked to name their academic major and the four-year institution to which they intend to transfer. At one campus, administrators were proud of faculty visibility, office hours, and offices located near classrooms, facilitating a strong, positive faculty-student interaction conducive to the transfer process. Administrators noted that many general education community college course credits are automatically transferable, which helps students move quickly to four-year institutions.

At low-transfer-rate colleges, administrators interviewed cited fewer *specific* programs and policies that encouraged students to transfer to four-year institutions. One administrator stated that students who received honors in high school could take community college courses during the summer months without a fee. In addition, one community college had established a program with a four-year institution where the student who had earned an associate's degree could have a baccalaureate degree program tailor-made to match his or her interests. The low-transfer-rate colleges were distinguished by discrepant responses to the interview questions, a diffused effort with many different programs, and an opportunistic attitude, especially when it came to retrieving extramural funds for all sorts of programs. They placed blame on outsiders, and made such comments as "the university doesn't want our students," and "the students' families are not interested in transfer." Many held the perception that transfer is just another function and exhibited no great concern one way or another for the transfer rates.

Administrators at both high- and low-transfer-rate campuses agreed that more could and should be done to assist students in meeting their transfer goals. Suggestions made by those interviewed included mandating common course numberings throughout all state institutions. In addition, stronger articulation agreements, more financial aid, and concurrent enrollment at both two- and four-year campuses would be of benefit. One person interviewed suggested that universities should accept most or all community college courses for transfer credit. At the very least, improved understanding and agreement between two- and four-year campuses should be established in order to decide what will be accepted for transfer to a university.

Summary

These data on transfer rates are useful for those who would assist students in navigating a chaotic system. Transfer, to use the example detailed in this chapter, does not happen automatically but is a function of college activities and the perceptions held by students and staff members. Student flow is a local responsibility; it seems only tangentially related to state policies.

Higher education operates with a great deal of internal inertia. Stasis in curriculum and role expectations, and the heavy hand of tradition act to retard the pace of change. The students' prior learning, the funding that comes from extramural sources, state mandates for interinstitutional articulation and for uniform graduation requirements, and federal goals for student-body representativeness all intrude. But one who would understand college outcomes should look to the single college as the unit of analysis. Easing student movement from one institution to another within a disorderly system presents a challenge.

References

American Association of State Colleges and Universities. *AASCU/Sallie Mae National Retention Project: 1993 Survey Results.* Washington, D.C.: American Association of State Colleges and Universities, 1994. (ED 380 019)

Cohen, A. M., and Brawer, F. B. *The American Community College.* (3rd ed.) San Francisco: Jossey-Bass, 1996.

Mabry, T. N. *A Study of the Differences in Transfer Rates Between Community Colleges and Four-Year Colleges in Fifteen States.* Unpublished dissertation, Graduate School of Education and Information Studies, University of California, Los Angeles, 1995.

National Center for Education Statistics. *Digest for Education Statistics 1995.* Washington, D.C.: U.S. Department of Education, 1995.

Orfield, G., and Paul, F. G. "State Higher Education Systems and College Completion." Final Report to the Ford Foundation, November 1992. (ED 354 041)

Smith, T. M., and others. *The Condition of Education 1994.* Washington, D.C.: National Center for Education Statistics, U.S. Department of Education, 1994. (ED 371 491)

ARTHUR M. COHEN is director of the ERIC Clearinghouse for Community Colleges and professor of higher education at the University of California, Los Angeles.

This chapter examines the discussion surrounding a reliable transfer rate measure by outlining the major arguments advanced by scholars and researchers in the field. Several traditional methods of calculating transfer rates are discussed and new ways of conceptualizing transfer rate definitions are introduced.

New Ways of Conceptualizing Transfer Rate Definitions

Frankie Santos Laanan, Jorge R. Sanchez

Measurement of the flow of student transfer from two- to four-year institutions is often used as an indicator of the community college's ability to fulfill its transfer function. Currently, there are many ways of defining a transfer rate and no defined methodology for calculating transfer rates. Few argue about the purpose and value of measuring transfer rates: to calculate the extent to which community colleges contribute to the educational progress of students en route toward the baccalaureate. However, agreeing on what constitutes a transfer rate is another matter.

Dilemmas of Calculating Transfer Rates

In simple terms, the calculation of a transfer rate involves decisions about which students to put into the numerator and denominator of a fraction. The numerator includes the number of students who have transferred to four-year institutions; the denominator is the number of students who could potentially transfer. The debate over which measures to use for the numerator and denominator in the transfer rate calculation is important because the outcome of the calculation is often used to represent the extent to which community colleges are productive and effective educational institutions. Fonte (1993) posits that any definition of a transfer rate would be sufficient if it were viewed only as an arithmetic measure of student movement between two segments of higher education. However, it is precisely because the transfer rate is used as a way to measure the effectiveness of community colleges that the definition becomes critical.

Efforts to estimate two-year college success in propelling students toward university entrance (or transfer) continues to be a challenging task among researchers in higher education (Cohen, 1991; McMillan and Parke, 1994). According to Cohen (1991), transfer rates have been reported from various sources and they rarely match because the data are inconsistent and the formulas used to calculate those rates vary. Similarly, Hirose (1994) argues that there is insufficient empirical data that accurately measure the transfer function. Problems of measurement include issues such as the inconsistent methods of transfer data collection among institutions and a lack of consensus on the definition of the formula employed to calculate student transfer (Cohen, 1991; Hirose, 1994; Palmer, 1986). Cohen (1991) found that the variety of formulas used to calculate transfer rates resulted in findings that ranged from 5 percent to 84 percent. In a more recent effort presented in this volume, Spicer and Armstrong suggest that there are eleven possible definitions of the transfer rate (see Chapter Five). Based on their evaluation of these eleven definitions, they maintain that because of the multiple options for defining the denominator in a transfer rate equation, researchers will derive different ratios of what constitutes transfer cohort success.

Overview of Traditional Transfer Rate Models

Transfer rates are important because they provide an answer to the question, What is the community college's contribution to its students' progress toward the baccalaureate? (Cohen, 1993). Numerous attempts have been made to measure the community college's contribution to its transfer mission. These studies have been conducted at the national, regional, state, and individual college levels. Each of these efforts has as its common objective to credit the community college for each student who effectively makes the journey from a community college to a four-year college or university. To date, the popular method of doing this has been to focus on tracking an entering student cohort through to the senior institution in order to determine the number who successfully transfer. The following is a synthesis of the traditional methods that have been used to calculate the number of students who transfer.

An early study conducted by Adelman (1988) used transcripts of students who participated in the National Longitudinal Study of the High School Class of 1972 as a method of calculating transfer rates. He estimated that 20 percent of the students who received bachelor's degrees had attended a community college at some point in their academic careers. Another method of calculating transfer is derived from a study conducted by Flaherty (1989). He defined transfer as the number of students transferring to an Illinois four-year college or university divided by the total enrollment in pre-baccalaureate programs during the previous fall. By his calculations the transfer rate was less than 12 percent for Illinois community colleges. At the same time as Flaherty conducted his study, the Chancellor's Office of the California Community Colleges (1989) calculated a transfer rate exceeding 42 percent by dividing the number of students transferring in 1988–89 by the number of California high school graduates who entered community colleges three years prior to transfer.

Another transfer definition measures the leavers from community colleges (Berman, Weiler and Associates, 1990). Working closely with the National Effectiveness Transfer Consortium (NETC), the model defines the potential transfer cohort as the number of students exiting the community college (number of leavers times one hundred). This method surveys students who enroll in a community college in a given term, complete at least six units there, and do not return to the community college the following fall. This definition excludes students who are enrolled concurrently in a four-year college or who possess a bachelor's degree. The time frame limits transfer to the period immediately after exiting the community college. The data collection process entails a follow-up survey of leavers or contacting cooperating four-year colleges directly. Berman, Weiler and Associates (1990) found that 26 percent of those who fit their definition matriculate to a four-year college or university.

The Ford Foundation Transfer Assembly, conducted by the Center for the Study of Community Colleges (CSCC), uses a different methodology for calculating transfer rates. Developed by Cohen (1991), this method tracks an *entering* student cohort. Now in its seventh year, the project has defined a valid way of calculating transfer that can be applied nationwide and has encouraged colleges, universities, and state agencies to report data according to that formula (Cohen, 1993, 1994). The overall intent was to build a consistent way of estimating the community college's contribution to its students' progress toward the baccalaureate. The CSCC model defines a transfer rate as "all students entering the community college in a given year who have no prior college experience and who complete at least twelve college-credit units, divided into the number of that group who take one or more classes at the university within four years" (Cohen, 1994, p. 73). For the last six years, the CSCC has yielded a national transfer rate average of 22 percent.

Most recently, McMillan and Parke (1994), from the Illinois Community College Board, adapted the NETC and Transfer Assembly models to calculate transfer rates for students enrolled in the Illinois public community college system. In their effort to operationalize the entering (Transfer Assembly) and exiting (NETC) cohort models for the Illinois transfer rate study, McMillan and Parke made two modifications. First, although the CSCC model includes all first-time students regardless of enrollment program, the Illinois study limited the definition to enrollments in baccalaureate-transfer, occupational, or general associate programs. Second, although the NETC model uses six credit hours as a minimum, the Illinois study raised the threshold from six to twelve, the credits were limited to college-level hours, and the cohort was limited to the same three programs as the entering cohort. McMillan and Parke's (1994) analysis revealed two rather different outcomes. The modified CSCC overall transfer rate was 20.1 percent, whereas the modified NETC overall fall transfer rate was 14.9 percent. Furthermore, when the rates were calculated by college-level programs, the findings showed differences in transfer behavior by program area. For example, four out of five students enrolled in the baccalaureate-transfer programs actually transferred to a senior institution. Variation in transfer rates by program supports similar findings in other studies (Fonte, 1993; Grubb, 1991; Illinois Community College Board, 1990, 1992).

Strengths and Weaknesses of Traditional Rate Models

The studies just mentioned reveal considerable variation in the transfer rate depending on the formula used. In the transfer equations, there is no common denominator or set of students being tracked. In addition, some calculations do not use the same numerator or subset of the original group being tallied over a specific period. This results in very different transfer rates, creates confusion, and raises questions about the meaning these rates have for community colleges and the public. An examination of the strengths and weaknesses of the traditional models further emphasizes the concerns about transfer rates and their reliability.

Although the U.S. Department of Education report (or Adelman's study) is useful and informative, it provides one transfer rate for a cohort of students within one particular time frame. Transfer rates from additional years beyond the 1972 cohort were not calculated. Both the Flaherty (1989) and California Community Colleges (1989) studies used cross-sectional measures instead of tracking students from the community college to the four-year institution. Because each used a different method of measuring the cross-sectional cohort, the resulting transfer rates were drastically different. A serious flaw in the Berman, Weiler and Associates study is that by measuring leavers it does not take into account that a student may be a leaver more than once and therefore may be counted more than once as a transfer (Cohen, 1991, Hirose, 1994). In contrast, the Transfer Assembly project collects longitudinal data in order to track students over a four-year period. Longitudinal studies like the Assembly's entering cohort model have been found to have greater validity for determining transfer rates than cross-sectional models like the leaver approach used by Berman, Weiler and Associates (Garcia, 1991). Not only does the Assembly model permit community college transfer behavior to be tracked, it also provides a measure of student persistence.

Given the strength of the Transfer Assembly model, some of the limitations should not be overlooked. The model omits students who do not transfer within the four-year time frame. A study conducted by Garcia (1992) shows that extending the time frame three or four years beyond the four-year limit adds up to 5 percent. Also, the model excludes private university transfers and out-of-state transfers. Because most data are collected from public institutions, the transfer rates will likely be depressed in states that have large numbers of students transferring to in-state private institutions (for example, New York).

In their adaptation of two national methodologies, McMillan and Parke (1994) found that two major differences in the transfer rate resulted when program of study and student intent were considered. Specifically, among entering and fall exiting students, those intending to transfer achieved the highest overall actual transfer rate at about 31 percent. In fact, when student intent and program areas were combined, data yielded the highest rates in the study in each program area. That is, transfer rates for students intending to transfer yielded higher overall rates within each individual program area. There is widespread agreement in support of the idea that student intent is important when deciding which individuals to include in transfer rate calculations (Clagett and Huntington, 1992; Fonte, 1993; Walleri, Seybert, and Cosgrove, 1992). However, researchers agree that gathering consistent and accurate data on intent to transfer can be problematic. For example, Cohen (1993) maintains that not all colleges ask students about their intentions. In addition, the way in which the question is framed severely biases the responses. Finally, students may alter intentions over time. However, despite the apparent weaknesses in considering student intent, McMillan and Parke, as a result of their study, suggest that adhering to one transfer definition may be limiting. They maintain that multiple transfer rates are necessary in order to help community colleges more effectively convey information on their diverse student populations.

Nontraditional Transfer Rate Models

The idea of using multiple transfer rates to convey information about student transfer and community college effectiveness has prompted some researchers to look at new ways of conceptualizing transfer rates. Boese and Birdsall (1994) presented their initial findings of a pilot study where they attempted to define the concept of transfer eligibility. They contend that "transfer rate measures to date have focused on the number of students who actually transfer—an outcome which is much more in the control of four-year institutions" (p. 11). Their presentation proposes a nontraditional approach to calculating the transfer rate and presents operational definitions of *transfer eligibility* and *transfer intent* that can be used by community college researchers with data from their own institutions. Boese and Birdsall defined the transfer eligibility rate as the ratio of transfer-eligible students to transfer-intent students. The focus is on the degree to which a group of first-time students with no prior college experience who indicate transfer to a four-year college or university as their educational goal are prepared by the community college to meet their objective.

Working from Birdsall and Boese's (1995) pilot work, Rasor and Barr (1995) developed an institutionally useful definition of students who reach transfer eligibility status. They propose a transfer eligibility rate that can be derived using *transfer eligible* as the numerator and *transfer directed* as the denominator. Rasor and Barr (1995) define *transfer eligible* as "students who earlier met the definition of transfer directed, and who also successfully completed fifty-six or more transfer-level units (or quarter unit equivalent) within a specified period of time, with a cumulative GPA of 2.0(C) or higher in those transfer courses." *Transfer directed* is defined as "new freshman students, without prior college units, who at any time during a specified enrollment period at the college, successfully complete ("C" or higher, using any grade of record) a transfer level English writing course (e.g., English 1A or ESL equivalent) as well as a transfer level math course, both of which satisfy the general education requirements in the California State University system" (p. 1).

From composite data for Fall 1987, 1988, and 1989, Rasor and Barr identified 10,782 students who enrolled at their colleges as first-year students with no prior college experience. Of these identified students, 1,667 (15.5 percent of the initial 10,782) successfully enrolled and completed both transfer-level English and math within four years of their initial enrollment. Only 1,114 (10.3 percent of the initial 10,782 students) were able to complete fifty-six or more transferable units and maintain a grade point average of 2.0 or higher. Thus the transfer eligibility rate for the composite three-year cohort would be 66.8 percent (1,114/1,667).

As a result of the aforementioned research, California community college institutional researchers proposed a transfer readiness rate as an appropriate measure of community college effectiveness (The Research and Planning Group, 1995). They contend that the use of current transfer rates, which focus on the actual number of students who transfer, underestimates the college's effort to ready a cohort of students to transfer. Their discussions have focused on measuring the college's ability to prepare students for transfer, rather than measuring those who do transfer. *Transfer readiness rate* is defined as the number of students who successfully complete specified transfer eligibility requirements, divided by the number of all transfer-directed students within a given time frame. This rate is intended to measure how well community colleges are preparing students to transfer.

An approach that considers transfer eligibility or transfer readiness as one of several measures formulated to indicate the success of community colleges in preparing students for transfer is presented by Baratta (1992). He developed a framework referred to as the Transfer Tracking System (TTS) in order to take a closer look at the transfer process and the role community colleges play in that process.

Baratta identified six types of transfer students. The first four transfer types are similar to the four transfer student cohorts (traditional, returning, reverse, and concurrent) defined in a study by Garcia (1992). What makes Baratta's study unique is the addition of two transfer types, one of which is an example of one form of transfer eligibility.

Traditional transfer (type one): first-year student at a community college
Returning transfer (type two): first-year student at a community college who transferred to a four-year institution, but then returned to a community college
Reverse transfer (type three): first-year student at a four-year institution who later enrolled at a community college as an undergraduate
Concurrent transfer (type four): undergraduate who is attending a four-year institution and a community college simultaneously
Other transfer (type five): student not falling into any of the above categories usually because of incomplete information
Transfer eligible admitted (type six): student who first enrolled in a Contra Costa Community College District (CCCCD) college, known to have become transfer eligible and admitted into a four-year system, but who for some reason did not enroll at the four-year system

The TTS identified 36,576 students who were served during the 1982–83 to 1989–90 period by both CCCCD and a select four-year institution: University of California (UC), California State University (CSU), or St. Mary's College. According to Baratta, 58.4 percent (or 21,354) were *traditional transfers*; 10.8 percent (or 3,954) were *returning transfers*; 12.9 percent (or 4,709) were *reverse transfers*; 14.0 percent (or 5,120) were *concurrent transfers*; and 3.9 percent (or 1,439) were *other transfers* who could not be classified because of incomplete record information.

Since the fall of 1989, California community colleges have been using a statewide management information system for federal and state reporting and accountability purposes. This information system, in conjunction with UC and CSU information systems, is capable of classifying the transfer types identified by Baratta (1992), which would allow community colleges to consider transfer eligibility and readiness as one of several measures of success depending on the question the community college is asking about the success of its transfer function. If community colleges obtained information on an annual basis about the number of accepted transferable units per student; that is, the number of units that count toward fulfilling lower-division work, there would be a greater understanding of the effectiveness of community colleges in making students eligible and ready to enroll in further study if they so choose. It is not only individuals who transfer, but the work they have accomplished that transfers, too. If the coursework does not articulate, the student cannot transfer.

Conclusion

There is a growing interest on the part of institutional researchers in investigating innovative ways to measure and understand the community colleges' contributions in transfer education. The studies mentioned earlier provide evidence of the discussions and efforts being put forth by researchers in an attempt to move beyond the traditional models of transfer and to investigate new ways to account for the ultimate contribution of community colleges. There is a need for community colleges and four-year institutions to understand the heterogeneous student population. By identifying different transfer types, community colleges can measure different forms of effectiveness that are often masked by the traditional transfer rate models.

The issues surrounding the transfer rate debate continue to attract lively discussion in higher education. Specifically, the methodology of developing a reasonable and appropriate method of calculating student transfer is in question. Although institutional researchers and state agencies continue to develop new definitions or build from existing definitions, the problem still exists. Because of the lack of a defined methodology of calculating transfer rates, differing rates continue to be generated and used to make inferences that are sometimes contradictory and often confusing to the public and the media. Because no one definition can possibly be universal, using "multiple indicators of institutional effectiveness" (American Association of Community Colleges, 1992) or "multiple transfer rates" (McMillan and Parke, 1994) has received popular attention and support. The underlying policy implication for employing more than one measure is the notion that the diverse populations served by community colleges require multiple measures of success.

References

Adelman, C. "Transfer Rates and the Going Mythologies: A Look at Community College Patterns." *Change,* 1988, *20* (1), 38–41.

American Association of Community Colleges. *Policy Statement on Institutional Effectiveness.* Washington, D.C.: American Association of Community Colleges, 1992.

Baratta, F. *Profile of District Transfers to the University of California, California State University, and St. Mary's College.* Contra Costa, Calif.: Community College District, Office of District Research, 1992. (ED 920 457)

Berman, P., Weiler, D., and Associates. *Enhancing Transfer Effectiveness: A Model for the 1990s.* Washington, D.C.: American Association of Community and Junior Colleges, 1990. (ED 324 050).

Birdsall, L., and Boese, L. (1995). "Transfer Eligibility: Further Refinements and Further Directions." Paper presented at the California Community Colleges 1995 Annual Conference, San Diego, Calif., March 1995.

Boese, L., and Birdsall, L. (1994). "Measuring Transfer Eligibility: Definitions, Procedures, and Initial Findings." Paper presented at the annual conference of the California Association of Institutional Research, San Diego, Calif., November 1994.

California Community Colleges. *Community College Transfer Performance.* Sacramento, Calif.: Chancellor's Office, California Community Colleges, 1989.

Clagett, C. A., and Huntington, R. B. (1992). "Assessing the Transfer Function: Data Exchanges and Transfer Rates." *Community College Review,* 1992, *19* (4), 21–26.

Cohen, A. M. (1991). *A Model for Deriving the Transfer Rate: Report of the Transfer Assembly Project.* Washington, D.C.: American Association of Community Colleges, 1991.

Cohen, A. M. "Analyzing Community College Student Transfer Rates." Paper presented at the annual meeting of the American Educational Research Association, Atlanta, Ga., 1993. (ED 354 940)

Cohen, A. M. (ed.). *Relating Curriculum and Transfer.* New Directions for Community Colleges, no. 86. San Francisco: Jossey-Bass, 1994.

Flaherty, R. "2-Year Colleges Fail Test." *Chicago Sun-Times,* Nov. 12, 13, 14, 1989.

Fonte, R. "The Transfer Rate Debate: Toward a Reasonable Measurement of Transfer Effectiveness." *Journal of Applied Research in the Community College,* 1993, *1* (1), 11–24.

Garcia, P. *Operationalizing the Transfer Function.* Los Angeles: California State University, Office of the Chancellor, Division of Analytic Studies, 1992. (ED 344 652)

Garcia, P. *Transfer Rates: Some Contrasts.* Unpublished paper, Division of Analytic Studies, California State University, Sacramento, 1991.

Grubb, W. N. "The Decline of Community College Transfer Rates: Evidence from National Longitudinal Surveys." *Journal of Higher Education,* 1991, *62* (2), 194–217.

Hirose, S. M. "Calculating Student Transfer Rates: The Transfer Assembly Project." *Community College Review,* 1994, *22* (1), 62–71.

Illinois Community College Board. *A Study of Fall 1980 Illinois Community College Freshmen Earning Baccalaureate Degrees from Illinois Public Universities (1980–1988).* Springfield, Ill.: Illinois Community College Board, 1990.

Illinois Community College Board. *Fall 1986 First-Time Community College Student Transfer Study.* Springfield, Ill.: Illinois Community College Board, 1992. (ED 344 624)

McMillan, V. K., and Parke, S. J. "Calculating Transfer Rates: Examining Two National Models in Illinois." *Community College Review,* 1994, *22* (2), 69–77.

Palmer, J. "Sources and Information: The Social Role of the Community College." In L. S. Zwerling (ed.), *The Community College and Its Critics.* New Directions for Community Colleges, no. 54. San Francisco: Jossey-Bass, 1986.

Rasor, R. A., and Barr, J. E. "The Transfer Eligible Rate: Longitudinal Results of a Companion Measure to the Transfer Rate." Paper presented at the annual conference of the Research and Planning Group for the California Community Colleges, San Diego, Calif., March 1995.

Research and Planning Group for California Community Colleges. "Transfer Readiness Rate: A Prototype Model. A New Approach to Measuring the Community College Transfer Function." *The Research and Planning Group Policy Paper,* Oct. 1995, pp. 1–3.

Walleri, R. D., Seybert, J. A., and Cosgrove, J. J. "What Do Students Want? How Should Intentions Affect Institutional Assessment? *Community, Technical and Junior College Journal,* 1992, 62 (4), 29–31.

FRANKIE SANTOS LAANAN is research associate at the Center for the Study of Community Colleges and a doctoral candidate in higher education at the University of California, Los Angeles.

JORGE R. SANCHEZ is director of institutional research at Coast Community College District and a doctoral student in higher education at the University of California, Los Angeles.

The authors demonstrate the disparate and highly political variability of the seemingly objective statistical measure of community college student transfer rates.

Transfer: The Elusive Denominator

Scot L. Spicer, William B. Armstrong

As important as the transfer function is to the community colleges, there remains a lack of consensus on a definition of a transfer rate (Banks, 1990, Cohen, 1987). Although it is generally agreed that the transfer rate is the ratio of students who transfer (numerator) to the potential number of transfer students (denominator), there is little agreement on what constitutes a potential transfer student, the denominator of all models. Suggestions as to the denominator have ranged from a college's total headcount, to those students completing at least a minimum number of units, to those students certified as transfer ready (that is, completing college- or university-specified lower-division general education requirements for the baccalaureate).

Although debate continues over the instructional priorities and effectiveness measures of the colleges, indicators of transfer effectiveness will most likely be integral to any state community college accountability system. For example, a recent report published by the Community College Roundtable of the American Association of Community Colleges (AACC), entitled *Core Indicators of Effectiveness in the Community Colleges,* included student transfer as one of the thirteen core measures of effectiveness. The final report of the Joint Commission on Accountability (JCAR), entitled *A Need Answered,* also included community college transfer rates as an essential accountability indicator. In California, the state model accountability system for community colleges includes student transfer as one of the mandated indicators of effectiveness.

Transfer Rate as an Indicator of Effectiveness

To be useful, a transfer rate indicator should provide a performance benchmark, be readily understood by a broad audience, be feasible in terms of time, cost, and expertise required to collect the information, and be a reliable statistic. However,

45

agreeing on a valid definition and a practical method of collecting reliable data has been among the most problematic aspects plaguing the adoption of a unitary transfer indicator (Clagett and Huntington, 1992; Brawer, 1991).

To further complicate the issue, not all transfer rates are equal. According to Kaagan and Coley (1989), the usefulness of an indicator rests on its ability to show what happens over time, what it can say about the performance of a college compared to another, and how the condition it measures compares with societal needs or expectations. Defining a transfer rate that meets these criteria has been difficult.

Defining Transfer: Same Questions, Different Answers

Underlying the broad interest in defining and describing student transfer is the question asked by lawmakers, journalists, and the public: how many community college students transfer to four-year colleges and universities? Although the question tends to be consistent, the answers can vary tremendously, as noted by Cohen (1990b). This is due to the variation in how transfer is defined and the availability of data to support the definition and answer the question.

Transfer data from California illustrates the problem. In California, although the state has three well-regarded postsecondary education systems (the University of California, California State University, and the California Community Colleges), there is little coordination on the issue of tracking students across the three segments. In 1990, the California Postsecondary Education Commission (CPEC) attempted a cross-sectional model to address the issues of transfer rate and defining the denominator. CPEC used the denominator options of total enrollment, total credit enrollment, full-time credit enrollment, and used first-time college students with in-state transfer for the year as the numerator. The data in Table 5.1 show how the potential transfer rates vary (from 3.7 percent to 17.7 percent) as the denominator is manipulated, with the numerator staying the same. Using these various definitions, the first column of the table, labeled *transfer pool*, refers to the number of students considered eligible for transfer, and although the number of transfers for that year remains constant, the transfer rate varies depending on the value of the denominator.

The data in Table 5.1 suggest the difficulty of interpreting the meaning of a transfer rate when there has been no agreement on a common definition. It also highlights the *political* problem of perceived low rates when broad cross-sectional approaches are used. The failure to agree on a unitary definition of transfer has made monitoring the community college contribution to student progress toward the baccalaureate problematic.

Once the pool of potential transfers has been identified, the question turns to how to calculate the transfer rate. For example, should the rate be cross-sectional (looking at a given group at one point in time), or longitudinal (following a cohort of potential transfer students from entry to transfer)?

The problem does not end with defining a transfer rate indicator. Once defined, obtaining the data to compute the rate has also been elusive (Brawer,

Table 5.1. Cross-Sectional Measures of Transfer Rates for California Community Colleges, 1982–1983

Transfer Pool	Transfers	Rate	Denominator
Total enrollment 1,354,949	50,537	3.7%	Credit and noncredit, new and continuing students
Credit enrollment 1,164,195	50,537	4.3%	Credit, new, and continuing students
Full-time credit 303,584	50,537	16.6%	Full-time credit, new, and continuing students
First-time freshmen 285,108	50,537	17.7%	Credit, first-time students

Source: CPEC (Report 90-23).

1991). For example, most current data collection practices in higher education rely on cross-sectional data, such as the number transferring in a given year from community colleges to senior institutions, rather than longitudinal data. According to Garcia (1991) and Adelman (1989), longitudinal data have greater validity than cross-sectional models when determining transfer rates. The current reliance on cross-sectional data makes meaningful and consistent transfer rate indicators difficult to define. The problem is described by Palmer and Eaton. "Few colleges array student data longitudinally to provide insights into the progress students make in college; where such longitudinal data sets are available, they are rarely tied to the information systems of four-year colleges and thus rarely provide information on either the proportion of students who transfer or their subsequent progress toward the baccalaureate. As a result, efforts to maximize transfer opportunities for minorities and others who use community colleges as an entrance to undergraduate higher education are based on untested assumptions rather than on evidence of what actually works" (1991, p. 24).

Similar questions were addressed in a report published in 1992 by the California Intersegmental Coordinating Council (ICC). This group, comprising representatives from the three public segments of California higher education (the University of California, California State University, and California Community Colleges) examined and compared several different transfer rate measures to recommend for adoption statewide. Among the cross-sectional approaches examined was the one developed by Berman, Weiler, and Associates (1990) and used by the National Effective Transfer Consortium (NETC). This method uses a nonreturning group of students (leavers) in a given term in the denominator and the number of transfers in the numerator (that is, number of transfers divided by number of leavers times one hundred). The NETC approach relies on surveys of nonreturning students to identify the percentage transferring to senior institutions. This method is thus highly dependent on student responses to follow-up surveys.

Various longitudinal approaches to calculating the transfer rate were also assessed by the ICC. These included the Transfer Assembly approach described in this article, and also a method developed by Lee and Frank (1990) in a study of transfer students at the City University of New York. Although the ICC did recommend some modifications, the Transfer Assembly definition was judged the most useful of the several transfer rate methods examined. This was primarily because of its reliance on a longitudinal approach to calculating transfer.

Definition questions of how best to count the transfer students have hindered efforts at arriving at a consistent rate. For example, in reviewing the ERIC database studies, Cohen (1990b) found transfer rates that ranged from 5 to 84 percent. The lowest rates were found in studies that divided the number of transfers into total college enrollment, and the highest rates were found where the number of transfers were divided by the number of students who had entered the colleges with intentions of transferring and had achieved some intermediate outcomes such as completing an associate's degree.

In addition to the general debate on the denominator, there have been specific objections to the various definitions. The inclusive nature of most denominator definitions has led many local campus leaders to request additional analyses that include only certain students in the denominator. For example, some believe that including students in the transfer-eligible pool who did not state transfer intent upon enrollment at the college was artificially lowering the transfer rate. However, others suggest that institutional practices might cause students to identify themselves as potential transfer students even when this was not their intention. This might occur in cases where students are not informed about the requirements and time it takes to transfer. Also, in some cases financial aid policies encourage students to indicate an intent to transfer to be eligible for aid. On the other hand, some institutions do not collect an educational intent from students. Others believe that student behaviors demonstrate intent and that the institution needs to have an adequate opportunity to mediate and inform the student's statement of intent before the student can be included in the transfer-eligible pool. Generally, however, community college leaders have been uncomfortable with studies to this point because their transfer rates were rather low numbers. To outside analysts, policy makers, and journalists, the reaction of community college leaders has been defensive on the topic of calculating and reporting transfer, because without some benchmark, no one could be sure how to interpret the numbers. This study attempts to clarify the importance of the denominator definition by comparing options suggested and thus providing the readers with an understanding of how denominator manipulation affects rates.

Methodology

Since 1988 the Transfer Assembly has been collecting and reporting data on community college transfers from a number of states across the country. Using a data-matching approach, participating community colleges prepare data files according to a specified definition developed by the Transfer Assembly and validated nationally over the last eight years. The cohort of students identified for matching with university enrollment files is defined by the Transfer Assembly as the number of students with no prior college experience who enter the community college and complete at least twelve credit units there within a four-year period. Using this definition, the CSCC has found that on average, of an entering cohort of first-time college students, nearly one-half complete at least twelve credit units, and of this group completing at least twelve credits, about one-quarter transfer within four years of their first community college enrollment.

This definition yields a transfer rate that has remained stable over time on a national level and on a state-by-state basis. This was found even with a dramatic increase in the number of participating colleges: from forty-eight in 1988 to over four hundred in 1995. These data have been found to provide both a well-recognized and a consistent indicator of student transfer, and were the basis for this study.

The source of the data for this study was the 1994 Transfer Assembly data for two community college districts. For the 1994 Transfer Assembly, both districts prepared data files that met the data elements and definitions required for participation in the data matching conducted by the CSCC. The four colleges included in the two districts were among the 395 community colleges that participated in the 1994 Transfer Assembly. A data tape of student ID numbers for the fall 1988 first-time cohort who completed twelve or more college credit units was matched against enrollment files for all of the California State Universities and University of California campuses by the CSCC. These matched files were returned to the respective districts under special agreement for this project where further analyses of the cohorts were conducted. The matched files gave each district transfer outcomes for specific students representing a large majority of their in-state transfers.

Choosing the Definitions

Denominators chosen for review initially came from models and approaches identifying student development and success found in the ERIC databases and other literature, a review of recent legislative mandates, and current discussions among researchers in the California community colleges about the absence of reliable transfer numbers. These denominators can be grouped into four categories. In the first are standard historical enrollment models (all new students, first-time college students, first-time students with a degree goal). In the second are those derived as policy exploration (Transfer Assembly, Student Right-to-Know). The third group of definitions were developed from discussion among California community college researchers frustrated by the lack of a reliable statistic focused on student behaviors (three possible versions of a *transfer ready* definition). Finally, the authors combined some of the historical models with observations of enrollment patterns and student outcomes. The eleven definitions are listed in Exhibit 5.1.

Exhibit 5.1. Possible Denominators for Calculating Transfer

Group A	All students new to the institution
Group B	All first-time college students
Group C	All first-time college students with a degree (AA, AS, certificate, baccalaureate) goal
Group TA	All first-time college students who earned at least twelve units in a four-year period (Transfer Assembly definition)
Group D	All first-time college students with a transfer goal
Group E	All first-time college students with a transfer goal and who earned more than zero units
Group F	All first-time college students with a transfer goal and who earned twelve or more units
Group SRK	All first-time college students with a degree goal who attempted full-time units in their first term (Student-Right-to-Know definition)
Group G	All first-time college students who are transfer-ready (completing freshman English composition and mathematics courses transferable to four-year colleges and universities)
Group H	All first-time college students with a transfer goal and who are transfer ready
Group I	All first-time college students with a transfer goal who are transfer ready and who have completed at least fifty-six units

Each of these definitions was applied to a group of transferring students identified in the Transfer Assembly data matching with the state enrollment files. This enabled comparison and evaluation of each of the proposed transfer definitions. Although the Transfer Assembly data do not include the state's private colleges and universities, they are the best data available to this date for California community colleges. Consequently, though imperfect, these data still highlight the issue of defining the denominator.

Transfer Ready

There has been a growing interest on the part of community college researchers, administrators, and faculty in determining the *transfer eligibility* rate for student cohorts. It is suggested that as a consequence of the changes in public policy toward higher education and fluctuations in regional economies, the dependent or criterion variable of student transfer to a four-year institution has become increasingly unstable from year to year. Thus, some suggest that community colleges can best communicate and document their success with students by analyzing the rate at which they prepare students to be ready to transfer, regardless of whether they actually transfer or not. It is suggested that this is an area over which the institution has control, and is more independent of the transfer policies, fee structure, or available seats at the local four-year college or university. Thus, it is more of a proximal rather than distal indicator. Community college researchers (Birdsall and Boese, 1995; Rasor and Barr, 1995) have proposed several transfer-ready models to evaluate the transfer function of community colleges. These models suggest that a transfer eligibility rate be calculated with a numerator of students who have demonstrated commitment to transfer by such actions as completing a transfer-level course in mathematics or English, by completing fifty-six or more transferable units, or by achieving a grade point average of 2.00 (C) or better (Groups G, H and I).

Transfer readiness as a concept appeared attractive because it was seen as an independent measure of community colleges' preparation of students for transfer not dependent on data from outside the community college. On the other hand, the transfer-readiness approach does seem to assume that all students will complete a similar set of requirements for transfer—this has not been validated by any of the proponents. In fact, the authors of the present study would conclude that students transfer to four-year institutions without completing two years of lower-division course work and without fulfilling some transfer requirements of the senior institutions depending on their enrollment needs at particular times. Thus, for purposes of this study only actual enrollment in a four-year institution is included in the numerator.

Student Right-to-Know/A Change in the Numerator Too

The authors of this project made a conscious decision to focus on the issue of the denominator in calculating transfer rates to evaluate the impact of various denominator definitions. One of the definitions to be evaluated is the federal Student Right-to-Know (SRK) formula, which in all likelihood will become an important benchmark. SRK reporting, however, initiates a somewhat broader interpretation of success than the restricted definition, enrollment in a four-year institution, that has been previously proposed in transfer definitions. SRK includes in its numerator those enrolling at a four-year institution, those who transfer to any other institution, those continuing enrollment, and those completing a (community college) degree or certificate at the initial institution. For purposes of this study, although we have included the SRK denominator definition, we are including only actual enrollment at a four-year institution in our numerator.

Findings

As has been discussed throughout this report, the transfer rate can vary considerably when conditions are applied to include particular students in the potential pool of transfer students. Figure 5.1 dramatically illustrates how the transfer rate increases with various conditions applied to the initial cohort or denominator. Although the transfer rate increases, however, the proportion of the initial cohort of students included as transfer eligible can decrease so much that a large majority of the institution's students are not included. Consequently, the use of a more specific transfer-rate definition may beg the public policy question we started with.

Figure 5.1. Cohort Size and Transfer Rate

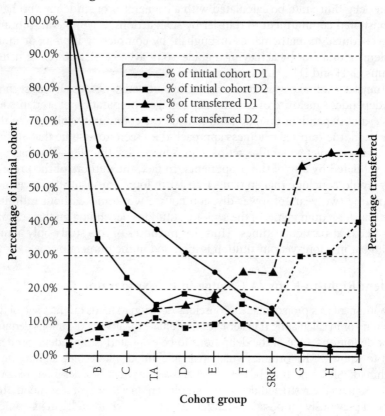

In the preceding example, the transfer rate varies from 5.3 percent to 61.3 percent for District 1 and from 3.6 percent to 40.4 percent for District 2. In each case, the lowest rate is with a denominator of *all new students* (A) and the highest rate came with the most exclusive transfer ready definition (I). For the most part, each district had an increasing transfer rate across the definitions, as ordered by the authors, corresponding to a declining proportion of the entering student cohort in the denominator. For example, whereas definition A—all new students—includes 100 percent of both districts' initial cohorts, the SRK definition includes 4.6 percent of the initial cohort from District 2 and 14.0 percent of District 1's initial cohort. Similarly, the transfer-ready denominators (G and H) only capture between 1.2 and 3.6 percent of the initial cohorts of the two districts.

Several other quirks become apparent as we look at the data. For example, other than the *all new students* (A) definition, none of the definitions captured more than half of all the transfers for District 2. District 1, on the other hand, had no fewer than 88 percent of their transfers captured in definitions B, C, D, E, and F. Further, 66 percent of all District 1 transfers were captured by the SRK denominator definition, whereas only 15 percent of District 2's transfers were captured by the SRK denominator definition.

The secondary question raised by this study, after understanding the impact of the denominator in a transfer rate formula, is, what definition best represents an institutional transfer rate for each district? Although some express dissatisfaction with models that included all students as potential transfers regardless of intent, inclusion of student intent to transfer as a condition for transfer eligibility seems to be less important than actual transfer-related behaviors such as completion of transfer-level English or math courses. Clearly there has been value added to the student as a result of successful completion of college-level English and math, particularly when preparing for employment in our increasingly information-based economy. The question then becomes more difficult. The data from this study suggest there are important questions to consider when we restrict entry into the denominator of a transfer-rate formula. Although we increase our transfer rate dramatically by restricting entry to only the most serious students, we risk a cynical response by legislators, the media, and community groups by severely limiting the potentially eligible pool of transfer students. Herein lies the fine art of policy making regarding accountability. Even the SRK definition (all first-time college students with a degree goal who attempted full-time units in their first terms), because it misses so many of the eventual transfers in one district, would not be a good singular choice for policy making for that district. Transfer rates, as with other educational indicators, are difficult to use both as a program accountability tool for external audiences and for local planning and program review purposes. Local college leaders need to review the various transfer-rate formulas and determine for themselves which best describe the role of their colleges in preparing students for transfer. For whom should the college take responsibility for transferring? The answer to this question seems to lie somewhere between the all-inclusive transfer-eligible pool and the most restrictive definitions of transfer-ready presented here.

References

American Association of Community Colleges. *Core Indicators of Effectiveness, AACC Special Reports No. 4, A Report of the Community College Roundtable*. Washington, D.C.: American Association of Community Colleges, 1994.

American Association of Community and Junior Colleges. *A Model for Deriving the Transfer Rate: Report of the Transfer Assembly Project*. Washington, D.C.: American Association of Community and Junior Colleges, 1991.

Adelman, C. "Using Transcripts to Validate Institutional Mission: The Community Colleges in the Post-secondary Experience of a Generation." Paper presented at the annual meeting of the Association for the Study of Higher Education, Atlanta, Ga., November 1989. (ED 313 963)

Banks, D. "Why a Consistent Definition of Transfer?" *Community College Review,* 1990, *18* (2), 47–53.

Berman, P., Weiler, D., and Associates. *Enhancing Transfer Effectiveness: A Model for the 1990's*. Washington, D.C.: American Association of Community and Junior Colleges, 1990. (ED 324 050)

Birdsall, L., and Boese, L. "Transfer Eligibility: Further Refinements and Further Directions." Paper presented at the annual conference of the Research and Planning Group for the California Community Colleges, San Diego, Calif., March 1995.

Brawer, F. B. "Bad News/Good News: Calculating Transfer Data." *Community College Review,* 1991, *19* (3), 48–53.

California Post-secondary Education Commission (CPEC). *Student Profiles 1990. The First in a Series of Annual Factbooks about Student Participation in California Higher Education.* Report 90-23. Sacramento, Calif.: California Post-secondary Education Commission, 1990. (ED 329 200)

Clagett, C. A., and Huntington, R. B. "Assessing the Transfer Function: Data Exchanges and Transfer Rates." *Community College Review,* 1992, *19* (4), 21–26.

Cohen, A. M. "The Transfer Indicator." Paper presented at the 70th annual convention of the American Association of Community and Junior Colleges, Seattle, Wash., April 1990a.

Cohen, A. M. "Counting the Transfers: Pick a Number." *Community, Technical, and Junior College Times,* April 24, 1990b.

Cohen, A. M., and Brawer, F. B. *The Collegiate Function of Community Colleges.* San Francisco: Jossey-Bass, 1987.

Garcia, P. "Transfer Rates: Some Contrasts." Unpublished paper, California State University Office of the Chancellor, Division of Analytic Studies, 1991.

Intersegmental Coordinating Commission. *Assessing the California Transfer Function: The Transfer Rate and Its Measurement. Conclusions of the Data Needs Task Force.* Sacramento, Calif., Intersegmental Coordinating Commission, 1992. (ED 346 896)

Joint Commission on Accountability Reporting. *A Need Answered: Recommendations of the Joint Commission on Accountability Reporting.* Washington, D.C.: American Association of Colleges, National Association of Land Grant Colleges and the American Association for Higher Education, 1985.

Kaagan, S. S., and Coley, R. *State Education Indicators: Measured Strides, Missing Steps.* Princeton, N.J.: Center for Policy Research in Education, Rutgers University Policy Information Center, Educational Testing Service, 1989.

Lee, V. E., and Frank, K. "Student Characteristics that Facilitate Transfer from Two-year to Four-year Colleges." *Sociology of Education,* July 1990, 178–193.

Palmer, J., and Eaton, J. "Building the National Agenda for Transfer." In *Setting the National Agenda: Academic Achievement and Transfer.* Washington, D.C.: American Council on Education, 1991.

Rasor, R. A., and Barr, J. E. "The Transfer Eligible Rate: Longitudinal Results of a Companion Measure to the Transfer Rate." Paper presented at the annual conference of the Research and Planning Group for the California Community Colleges, San Diego, Calif., March 1995.

SCOT L. SPICER *is director of institutional research at Glendale Community College, California.*

WILLIAM B. ARMSTRONG *is director of institutional research at San Diego Community College and a doctoral student in higher education at the Graduate School of Education and Information Studies, University of California, Los Angeles.*

Current events deeply influence educational institutions. New collaborative articulation and transfer programs between two- and four-year institutions may be required to best meet the educational needs of students.

Moving Toward Collaboration in Transfer and Articulation

Dorothy M. Knoell

Attempts to provide a national perspective in which to propose changes in transfer and articulation are limited by the wide diversity of types of two-year institutions in the fifty states, and by ongoing changes in their mission (Adelman, 1992; Witt, Wattenbarger, Gollattscheck, and Suppiger, 1994). This limitation is compounded by a lack of information about transfer students that goes beyond the computation of rates of transfer (Cohen, 1993; Grubb, 1991). Furthermore, there are a number of trends that are probably affecting the size and nature of pools of potential transfer students, including: improved high school preparation for four-year college admission; questions about the propriety of affirmative action and other outreach programs to assist students who have been historically underrepresented in higher education; higher university admission standards; higher university costs, together with uncertainty about the availability of student financial aid; and increasing emphasis on vocational and technical education at the high school and community college levels, including new school-to-career programs.

Approaching the Twenty-First Century

Three or so decades ago, the typical community college transfer student was a recent high school graduate whose goal was a baccalaureate degree, but who enrolled in a two-year institution for one or two years after high school, or until he or she completed lower-division work (Knoell and Medsker, 1965). Such students usually had decided on their major field of study and the institution to which they intended to transfer by the time they began work in what were then junior colleges, and made steady progress in a two-plus-two program so as to transfer at the upper-division level and complete their baccalaureate-degree program in two or three years.

This traditional transfer group has been enlarged and diversified by affirmative action programs with the goal of achieving educational equity—more students from low income families, none of whose members had college experience; more Asian, black, Latino, and Native American students, many of whom graduated from low-performing schools, with families whose educational attainment was low; and students with limited or no English-language skills (Richardson and Bender, 1987).

Now, as the twenty-first century approaches, the potential transfer pool is being further enlarged by other types of what might be called nontraditional students, including the unemployed, displaced workers, and those whose skills need upgrading; welfare recipients who are required to go to school or work as a condition of receiving further benefits; women reentering higher education after a hiatus for homemaking and child-rearing, many of whom will be seeking employment for the first time; and some who might be called *interrupted scholars* with diverse interests, objectives, and educational backgrounds. Speculation about their interest in and potential for earning a baccalaureate degree, and the projection of numbers who will need access to transfer opportunities, are at best a challenge for planners for the next several decades.

The Need for New Opportunities to Transfer

One potentially large transfer population that is not now well served, if it is served at all, is the cohort of adults with an associate degree or its equivalent in a career or technical field who have been in the workforce and need upgrading, retraining, or simply validation of the skills they have learned on the job as they move up their career ladders. Their needs may now be met by community colleges in noncredit classes or contract education programs that employers arrange and fund, or by training provided by employers in which higher education institutions may not participate at all. However, there is now reason to suggest that new upper-division programs need to be developed to meet the special career advancement needs of working adults with less than a baccalaureate degree, whose earlier coursework in a community college was not intended for transfer. They have graduated from and been employed in various technical fields, and are now needed in and wish to move into middle-management jobs that require new kinds of skills and knowledge. The potential payoff is both to the workforce, which needs managers who have had work experience as technicians and education in management, and to workers who are ready for advancement into supervision and management.

Another justification for an increase in opportunities at the baccalaureate-degree level derives from pressures on community colleges to expand their credit-course offerings beyond the two-year associate's degree without themselves becoming four-year colleges. New instructional technology now makes it possible for baccalaureate-degree-granting institutions to provide students with access to upper-division work without their having to transfer physically. It frees students and faculty from the rigidities of time and place that are associated with on-campus instruction, where class scheduling is tied to the clock and the calendar. Technology facilitates distance learning, thus enabling workers to take courses at sites, including both the workplace and nearby community college campuses, and at times that are convenient to them, alone at their own pace, or in cooperative learning groups.

Community colleges themselves could benefit from a still different kind of transfer opportunity, which would prepare their graduates to become faculty and staff in high schools and two-year institutions, particularly in the technologies. What is envisioned is a new two-plus-two-plus-two program, which begins in a community college, leads to transfer, and continues on to an appropriate master's degree for teaching. It would include work experience for credit, built into the program at either or both the point of transfer and the point of entrance into the master's degree program. Cutbacks in state funding have led to the downsizing of traditional baccalaureate-degree programs that prepare high school and college vocational instructors. This downsizing has created problems for those who need at least a baccalaureate degree to teach, but it also provides an incentive for colleges and universities to develop new approaches to preparing community college faculty for technical programs.

School-to-work programs, which are being developed in secondary schools under the federal School-to-Work Opportunities Act of 1994, will need new kinds of staff. These may well be people who earn an associate's degree in a career field, gain significant work experience, and then complete a new kind of baccalaureate degree. It would be designed to prepare them to work cooperatively with schools, business, and industry in establishing school-to-work programs for high school students who may possibly continue their career education in a community college.

The federal government has been providing funds through the Carl D. Perkins Vocational and Applied Technology Act to develop two-plus-two-plus-two (six-year) career education programs that begin in the junior and senior years of high school and lead through the community college to a baccalaureate degree (Rancho Santiago Research Center, 1991; California Postsecondary Education Commission, 1987, 1992b). Programs being developed should but often have not included models that make provision for students to *stop out* for related work experience at various transition points during the six-year educational experience, ideally with degree credit granted for such experience. New emphasis on high school-through-community college *tech prep* programs, which are funded under the same federal act, may lead to decreased interest in six-year programs leading to a baccalaureate degree, particularly for experienced workers (Parnell, 1985). The issue remains of how best to serve adults in the workforce who possess less than a baccalaureate degree, but who need and are capable of achieving higher levels of collegiate education that would advance them in (or change) their careers.

New Approaches to Articulation: A Collaborative Model

The traditional approach to articulation involves faculty and staff in four-year institutions reviewing courses and programs from feeder community colleges, in order to make a judgment about their transferability and the baccalaureate-degree requirements they might meet, either as elective credit or in satisfaction of particular general education or major requirements. The community college may be asked to submit course syllabi or other information about the nature of the courses they offer, and may be permitted to appeal a negative decision about the transfer status of particular courses. Typically there is a limit of between sixty and seventy semester units on the amount of credit that may be transferred from a community college, and courses generally meet only lower-division requirements (Knoell, 1990a).

The process works best for recent high school graduates who enroll in only one community college and transfer without a significant lapse in time, but it may impede the progress of the increasingly diverse pool of potential community college transfer students, because of its rigidity. Enrollment in several community colleges in the course of completing a transfer program, concurrent enrollment in either two community colleges or in both a community college and a four-year institution, *stopping out* to work from time to time, and course-taking in a proprietary school all create articulation problems for students that the traditional approach does not currently solve.

Statewide common course numbering by community colleges, or by four-year institutions and their feeder community colleges, is one approach to simplifying the articulation of courses, but it is a complex, expensive process that does not obviate the need for the articulation of specific programs (California Postsecondary Education Commission, 1984). The development of common course numbers requires some degree of collaboration among faculties from the various disciplines in which the courses are to be articulated, but the number of faculty members who can be thus involved is limited by cost and the need to maintain teaching schedules while serving on statewide committees to develop such numbers. Furthermore, such a process tends to discourage faculty from making major changes in the content of, or in the way they teach, the courses that are in the common course numbering system.

For students who do not fit the traditional transfer-student model, a better collaborative model is one that involves the students, their faculty from the two- and four-year institutions, and their employers, working together to enable students to move toward their degree and career goals with ease between and among these institutions and the workplace. The concept of collaboration as an integral part of transfer and articulation was used in the report of a national study that the Ford Foundation funded several years ago (Knoell, 1990b). Evaluation of some type of portfolio or detailed resume appears to be more useful than simply an analysis of transcripts, particularly for students whose enrollment and work experience extend over a longer period of time than that of more traditional students.

Whereas a portfolio or resume would include such transcripts, it might also contain information about employment since high school and an accounting by the student of his or her life experiences that appear to be relevant to the individual's educational and career goals. Acceptance (or transfer) into an upper-division program may also require a formal assessment of skills that are critical to success in the program, for example, writing, oral communication, computer literacy, and mathematics skills. Collaborative articulation then takes on a kind of holistic quality, as faculty members evaluate how far the candidate has progressed in achieving his or her goals and objectives, and what he or she has yet to do in order to qualify for a baccalaureate degree. The prescription might include an internship or additional work experience, as well as course work that would either broaden his or her general education or satisfy graduation requirements in a major field. Where appropriate, some of the additional course work might be taken at a community college, at the workplace, or by distance learning, as well as on the campus of the institution that awards the degree.

This collaborative approach to articulation is student- rather than institution-centered, and is likely to be more efficient and effective than the more traditional process, at least from the student's point of view. It assumes that people learn from different kinds of experiences, at different rates, and in varying combinations of education and work. It needs to be a dynamic process, as students progress toward their goals, with adjustments made as experience is accrued.

Other Possibilities for Collaboration Among Faculties and Institutions

The discussion of collaborative articulation has dealt thus far with a process for moving individual students through their college enrollment and career experiences, toward the achievement of a baccalaureate degree. There are other possibilities for collaboration between two- and four-year institutions that should benefit potential transfer students, some of which are best suited to students who enter college directly after high school. The first involves joint admission to both a community college and a four-year institution, with transfer guaranteed to those who complete a lower-division transfer program with satisfactory grades. Such a policy might also include the joint awarding of associate's and bachelor's degrees. It enhances the reputation of the community college as an institution of higher education among parents and students alike, and gives assurance of access when the four-year institution is faced with a limitation on enrollment.

A second area of collaboration involves agreement on the assessment of future students' verbal and mathematical skills, with both types of institutions agreeing to the same assessment instruments and standards for determining readiness for college-level work. This joint activity presupposes agreement among faculties on the kinds and levels of skills that are essential for successful college work, and the involvement of secondary school teachers in incorporating them as objectives in their college-preparatory courses. Ideally, the assessment is conducted while potential college students are still in high school, with the intent that they may overcome any deficiencies before entering college. Collaboration among faculties is also called for as remedial instruction is designed and then offered to students who need it.

Collaboration in establishing general education requirements for graduation is still another way to facilitate articulation and speed the progress of transfer students toward the baccalaureate degree. This is in lieu of the traditional approach whereby faculty in four-year institutions virtually dictate what the general education program of the community colleges should be. Such collaboration is most effective when all public institutions in a state are able to agree on the nature of a majority of these requirements, the need for community colleges to teach them at the lower-division level, and the specific community college courses that will satisfy each of the requirements.

Fiscal constraints are making it increasingly difficult for students to enroll in one institution for all the courses they need in order to make steady progress to the degree. Thus collaboration may take the form of agreements for concurrent or cross-registration of students in community colleges and four-year institutions. Although community college courses will not usually qualify for upper-division credit, upper division students often are able to find community college courses that satisfy graduation requirements, either in regular or summer sessions. Still another aspect of this kind of collaboration involves the provision for high school juniors and seniors to earn college credit that advances them toward an associate's or bachelor's degree, either in a College Board Advanced Placement program or in college courses, which may be offered in the high school or on a college campus. Collaboration among faculties is important here because students are most likely to enroll at a conveniently located community college, with an expectation that the institution they will later enter as a first-year or transfer student will accept the college credit thus earned (California Postsecondary Education Commission, 1992a).

Fiscal constraints may also promote collaboration that involves the joint use of facilities and staff by nearby two- and four-year institutions (California Postsecondary Education Commission, 1992b). Examples of facilities that may be suitable for joint use include libraries, laboratories, athletic facilities, and facilities for the performing arts. Examples of staff who might be used jointly are instructors in remedial and English-as-a-Second Language programs, counselors, staff in outreach programs to high schools and the community, and other student services personnel. Staff such as articulation officers may be jointly employed, and the services of others, such as instructors in remedial programs, may be obtained under contract with the employing institution. Although budgetary conditions may be the motivation for such collaboration, increased contacts among faculty and staff in different types of institutions may be beneficial to transfer students as well.

A sixth area of collaboration is the joint development of courses that are taught in what may still be regarded as nontraditional modes, in order to increase the likelihood that institutions will award regular credit to students who enroll in them. Available instructional media are expanding beyond televised courses and media computerized instruction. Collaboration among faculty in both developing and teaching courses under conditions other than lecture hall instruction may increase their quality and should increase their mutual acceptability in meeting degree requirements.

Finally, professional development programs offer an opportunity for collaboration among faculties, which is likely to improve both teaching and learning, and articulation and transfer between two- and four-year institutions. In traditional programs, faculty in four-year institutions impart their knowledge and skills to community college instructors in a mentor and mentee relationship. In others, a community college offers a program for its own faculty, bringing in outside experts as needed. A collaborative program views the two faculties in a peer relationship, with common needs for staff development to improve teaching and learning, and the potential for making different kinds of contributions to the process. Examples of foci for collaborative activities that have potential to improve articulation are teaching and learning styles, curriculum content and sequence, and assessment of outcomes.

Governmental Developments of Concern

At present there is a considerable degree of uncertainty about the future of various governmentally funded programs that affect opportunities for transfer, at least indirectly. Such programs include affirmative action and outreach, student financial aid, workforce education and training, and welfare. At issue is both their level of funding and the commitment or opposition of legislators and others to them. Some potential actions might be expected to promote transfer, whereas others could hinder it or discourage enrollment in college at all.

Affirmative action. Pressures to *end or mend* affirmative action in the admissions practices of institutions of higher education may result in the diversion of students of color from four-year institutions to community colleges with open admission policies. One factor that would contribute to this diversion is a proposed ban on admissions to baccalaureate institutions based on racial and ethnic factors, which would affect both qualified applicants who are competing for a limited number of spaces and the small number who are now admitted in exception to requirements. A second factor would likely be reduced eligibility for regular admission to baccalaureate institutions as a result of new limits on the offering of special programs to reach out to and prepare high school students from groups that have been historically underrepresented in higher education. Finally, the probability of success for those who may still enroll would be reduced by a ban on specially targeted support programs and services, and the eventual elimination of remedial instruction in four-year institutions.

If these actions occur, the probable volume of diversion to or transfer from community colleges for those who would be denied admission as freshmen to four-year institutions cannot be projected with much certainty. Community colleges will be no more able than four-year institutions to offer special programs for disadvantaged students of color, and thus their potential for transfer may be lessened. Another option for some of these students is enrollment in a historically black institution, but the least favorable option is not to go to college at all.

Student financial aid. As noted earlier, uncertainty about the future availability of federally subsidized financial aid, together with increasing costs of attending public universities, may affect transfer in several ways. Students may be more likely to attend a community college as freshmen, because of uncertainty about financial aid; they may also be less likely to transfer, if federal grants and loans are not available on favorable terms. Finally, financial aid programs that have been specially targeted to racial and ethnic minorities may be eliminated as part of a larger movement to ban affirmative action.

Workforce education and training. Prospective changes in federally funded workforce education and training programs are likely to affect transfer and articulation in ways that are difficult to predict at this time. New federal legislation may combine funding for all workforce education and training into one block grant for states to distribute to providers, as each state sees fit. If community colleges increase their already strong role in workforce training as a result of this move, then the transfer function may well become less dominant. If, on the other hand, they were to lose the federal funding they now receive under the Perkins Vocational and Applied Technology Act and other federal training programs, then emphasis on the transfer function might increase as a means of maintaining enrollments. In any case, increased collaboration among educational institutions at all levels, as well as collaboration with business and industry, will be necessary to ensure the development of a world-class workforce.

Welfare reform. Whatever form welfare reform takes in the various states, the education and training of welfare recipients for employment is likely to be prominent. As in the case of workforce education, the future role of community colleges in performing this function is still uncertain. There is almost no likelihood that welfare recipients would be funded for more than two years of education leading to employment. However, some recipients may well be able to demonstrate their academic potential in a two-year program and should be able to transfer into a baccalaureate-degree program at some time in their career.

Conclusion

A good education for all Americans is among the nation's highest priorities, to ensure not only that the country will have a first-class workforce, but also that each individual will have an opportunity for education to achieve his or her full potential. Community colleges have done much to achieve this goal, without regard to an individual's socioeconomic status, racial or ethnic background, or gender. Much remains to be done to ensure that the needs of both the workers and the workforce are being met. A major thrust of this chapter has been to make a case for broadening the concepts of transfer and articulation, so as to make new opportunities available to new pools of potential students in the workforce that will enable them to enroll in appropriate baccalaureate-degree programs as they move up the career ladder.

This opening up of opportunities to complete a baccalaureate degree should not mean a lowering of standards or a lessening of the value of the degree. Instead, through increased collaboration among faculties and institutions, and with business and industry, it should mean a broadening and diversification of opportunity that will better serve the needs of the ever more diverse population of this country. The success of the transfer function should not be judged by volume or rates of transfer but, instead, by movement toward a vision of a future in which individuals who have successfully completed two years of postsecondary education or its equivalent will have an appropriate opportunity to continue their education toward a higher degree.

References

Adelman, C. *The Way We Are: The Community College as American Thermometer.* Washington, D.C.: U. S. Government Printing Office, 1992. (ED 338 269)

California Postsecondary Education Commission. *Common Course-Numbering Systems: A Report to the Legislature in Response to Senate Bill 851 of 1983.* (Commission Report 84–34) Sacramento, Calif.: California Postsecondary Education Commission, 1984. (ED 254 137)

California Postsecondary Education Commission. *Articulating Career Education Programs from High School Through Community College to the Baccalaureate Degree. A Report to the Governor, Legislature, and Educational Community in Response to Assembly Bill 3639.* (Commission Report 87–48) Sacramento, Calif.: California Postsecondary Education Commission, 1987.

California Postsecondary Education Commission. *Postsecondary Enrollment Opportunities for High School Students.* (Commission Report 92–13) Sacramento, Calif.: California Postsecondary Education Commission, 1992a.

California Postsecondary Education Commission. "Articulated Career Education Programs (2 + 2 + 2): One Approach to Career Development." Unpublished Commission report, August 1992b.

Cohen, A. "Analyzing Community College Student Transfer Rates." Paper presented at the annual meeting of the Association for Institutional Research, Chicago, May 1993.

Grubb, W. N. "The Decline of Community College Transfer Rates." *Journal of Higher Education,* 1991, 62, 194–217.

Knoell, D. M. "Guidelines for Transfer and Articulation." *Community, Technical, and Junior College Journal,* 1990a, 38, 41.

Knoell, D. M. *Transfer, Articulation, and Collaboration: Twenty-Five Years Later.* Washington, D.C.: American Association of Community and Junior Colleges, 1990b. (ED 318 528)

Knoell, D. M., and Medsker, L. L. *From Junior to Senior College: A National Study of the Transfer Student.* Washington, D.C.: American Council on Education, 1965.

Parnell, D. *The Neglected Majority.* Washington, D.C.: The Community College Press, 1985.

Rancho Santiago Research Center. *Third Party Evaluation of 2 + 2 + 2 Articulated Career Education Programs.* Santa Ana, Calif.: Rancho Santiago College, 1991.

Richardson, R. C., Jr., and Bender, L. W. *Fostering Minority Access and Achievement in Higher Education.* San Francisco: Jossey-Bass, 1987.

Witt, A., Wattenbarger, J. L., Gollattscheck, J. F., and Suppiger, J. E. *America's Community Colleges: The First Century.* Washington, D.C.: American Association of Community Colleges, 1994. (ED 368 415)

DOROTHY M. KNOELL has retired as chief policy analyst from the California Post-secondary Education Commission, and is currently a consultant in higher education.

Deliberations between faculty at two-year and four-year colleges can do much to articulate curricula, thereby enhancing transfer opportunities for community college students. But facilitating these deliberations will require radical departures from the traditions of classroom isolation that too often characterize faculty work.

Transfer as a Function of Interinstitutional Faculty Deliberations

James C. Palmer

Community colleges play several roles in baccalaureate education, that component of the educational continuum that links secondary education with graduate school and that leads to the award of the bachelor's degree. Providing access to undergraduate study is obviously one role. Conveniently located within commuting distance of most citizens, community colleges are a relatively low-cost alternative to the lower division of the university, and they are often the only point of entry for students whose academic backgrounds make them ineligible for university admission. By the same token, community colleges serve as a screen for the university, allowing society to keep the doors of undergraduate study open without requiring universities to abandon selective admissions; universities can be universities largely because of the system of community colleges that surrounds them. Finally, community colleges augment the university curriculum for many students who, though matriculated at the university, take one or two community college courses to fill out their programs of study.

Given the significant community college role in undergraduate education, Eaton's (1990) call for an academic approach to student transfer and curriculum articulation is highly practical. Student movement between colleges makes the two-year and four-year sectors interdependent; the work of the former affects the work of the latter and vice versa. The academic approach thus requires "collaborative work between two-year and four-year college faculty at the point of course development so that curriculum content and performance expectations are understood by both institutions and do not constitute unintended barriers to transfer" (Palmer and Eaton, 1991, p. 39). A key assumption is that faculty in both sectors will view the development of undergraduate education as a shared task. Rather than relying solely on articulation agreements and counseling services to help students move between institutions that construct undergraduate curricula internally and autonomously, the academic approach views curriculum itself as a key unifying factor and hence joint curriculum deliberations as an important articulation task.

How should these deliberations proceed? As a practical matter, they will need more structure than the deliberations of national blue-ribbon commissions that, as Kimball (1990, p. 95) points out, "avoid facing difficult trade-offs" by recommending "everything that any member believes is important" and that emphasize laudable and recurrent ideals, such as the need to improve student literacy skills, inculcate multicultural values in students, build a sense of community on campus, encourage a sense of student involvement, offer more coherent curricula, and enhance the importance of teaching within the university. Rather, the deliberations should structure the work of faculty members who carry out the undergraduate program. With this end in mind, two-year and four-year college educators might focus their deliberations around three themes: the formal structure of the undergraduate curriculum—that is, the types and arrangement of courses that students are required to complete; course content and learning objectives, both in terms of disciplinary knowledge and general education; and faculty roles and responsibilities. Decisions made in each of these areas will affect the character of the undergraduate program and the respective roles played by the two-year and four-year college.

The Formal Curriculum

At one level, undergraduate education can be studied as a system of courses. Veysey (1990, p. 175) calls this "formal" curriculum "a highly complicated series of structural arrangements, embodying many separate kinds of routine understandings." It is these understandings, he notes, that make the college experience familiar to us. Students take courses that are sponsored by academic departments, offered for set periods of time (quarters or semesters), and culminate in grades and the award of credit. There are protocols for the number of courses required for the baccalaureate and for their distribution, some fulfilling the requirements of the major, some fulfilling general education requirements, and others taken as electives. Although this outward structure says little about academic substance and quality, it has been a relatively stable part of American higher education since the emergence of the university—from which it arose—in the 1890s. Veysey observes that whereas colleges and universities have changed considerably since 1900, the skeletal design of the undergraduate curriculum has not.

Articulation and transfer have been well served by this consistency. The peculiarly American idea of discreet courses for which students earn transportable semester-hour credit facilitates student mobility between institutions, making the community college *as college* possible. And although transfer students sometimes find their progress impeded by discrepancies between the formal curricula of the community college and the university, both institutions at least share a common currency of exchange and a common language of negotiation. These shared understandings are reflected in articulation agreements. The transfer admission agreements (TAAs) for community college students who plan to attend the University of California, Davis, are an example. As Knoell (1994; p. 133) explains, each "TAA is a formal, written agreement that outlines the courses a student must take before transferring, states the GPA a student must earn, and lists specific requirements for limited access majors. After a TAA is written, the student signs the agreement, along with . . . a Davis campus representative. These signatures guarantee that the student will be admitted to Davis in the major and for the term of choice, provided the student fulfills the agreement."

In constructing these agreements, two-year and four-year college educators help shape the structure if not the substance of the undergraduate experience. Sometimes small but irritating problems require attention. Some of the projects funded by the Ford Foundation's National Center for Academic Achievement provide illustrations. For example, faculty members from Georgia State University and Atlanta Metropolitan College compared their mathematics curricula, attending to differences between the two institutions in the ways courses were sequenced from developmental mathematics through calculus. Because of these differences, Atlanta Metropolitan students sometimes lost credit if they transferred to Georgia State prior to completing the full sequence (Najee-ullah and others, 1993).

But in other cases, larger, perennially-debated issues are addressed. One is general education. Here ongoing discussions about which courses fulfill general education requirements are moved from the institutional arena to the interinstitutional arena. A second issue deals with prescription and the question of whether students should be required or urged to complete two years of study at the community college before transferring to the university.

General Education. Some interinstitutional deliberations are initiated to identify courses that meet commonly agreed upon curricular goals, particularly in general education. The Illinois Board of Higher Education (IBHE), for example, has begun a statewide articulation initiative involving faculty from two-year and four-year colleges in the development of model lower-division curricula. The first product of the initiative, a transferable general education curriculum, was released for comment in 1993 and endorsed by the IBHE and the Illinois Community College Board in 1994 (Illinois Board of Higher Education, 1994). It defines the purpose of general education, specifies a thirty-seven to forty-one semester-hour sequence of courses in five areas (communications, mathematics, humanities and fine arts, social and behavioral sciences, and physical and life sciences), and delineates the competencies students are to demonstrate in each (See Exhibit 7.1.).

More than 100 two-year and four-year college faculty members from each of the five disciplinary areas represented in the model curriculum contributed to its development through a year-long process of task-force deliberations. Colleges

Exhibit 7.1. Illinois General Education Core Curriculum Requirements

Communications	Three courses (nine semester credits), including a two-course sequence in writing (six semester credits) and one course (three semester credits) in oral communication
Mathematics	One to two courses (three to six semester credits)
Physical and Life Sciences	Two courses (seven to eight semester credits), with one course selected from the life sciences and one course from the physical sciences and including at least one laboratory course
Humanities and Fine Arts	Three courses (nine semester credits), with at least one course selected from humanities and at least one course from the fine arts
Social and Behavioral Sciences	Three courses (nine semester credits), with courses selected from at least two disciplines
Total	Twelve to thirteen courses (thirty-seven to forty-one semester credits)

Source: Illinois Board of Higher Education, 1994, p. 5.

are expected to identify courses within their curricula that lead to the specified competencies; it is expected that students who complete these courses and transfer to another Illinois college or university will not be required by the receiving institution to complete additional general education courses at the lower division.

The Illinois articulation initiative was significant in that it formalized discussions between two-year and four-year college faculty members who had heretofore interacted on an occasional basis. It is an open question, though, how far participants in these types of deliberations are willing to go to restructure the undergraduate experience. For example, the Illinois general education sequence outlined in Exhibit 7.1 does not mention interdisciplinary courses or other alternatives to the familiar approach of fulfilling general education requirements by completing elective courses. Although it is conceivable that individual colleges might structure interdisciplinary courses to meet the core requirements, the specification of courses in individual disciplines does little to promote experimentation with transferable forms of general education that depart from the norm.

Prescription. Another broader issue that might be addressed in deliberations about the formal curriculum lies in the question of prescription. *Within* individual colleges, deliberations about prescription center on how much leeway students should have in designing their programs of study (Veysey, 1990). Deliberations *between* institutions may add the question of whether students should be allowed to transfer at any point during their community college experience, or whether they should be encouraged to complete a specified portion of the undergraduate curriculum before transferring.

Articulation policies often lean to the latter. State policies in both Illinois and Florida, for example, tie articulation to the completion of the associate's degree, guaranteeing junior status to community college students who earn credentials in collegiate areas. The effects vary. In Florida, where articulation guidelines are written into the state's education code and are augmented by a common course-numbering scheme and other articulation aids, approximately 69 percent of the students transferring from community colleges to the state's university system in the late 1980s did so with associate's degrees (Belcher and Baldwin, 1991). In Illinois, which has an articulation compact that colleges and universities adhere to voluntarily rather than by legal mandate, the proportion of transfer students in the late 1980s who held associate's degrees was only 44 percent (Illinois Board of Higher Education, 1992).

More recently, some states have tied articulation to transferable general education or liberal arts modules that represent system-wide expectations for lower-division achievement short of the associate's degree. The Illinois general education module discussed above is an example. In Virginia, the State Board for Community Colleges has joined the Virginia State Council of Higher Education in endorsing a transfer module consisting of thirty-five semester hours of specified arts and sciences courses to be offered throughout the Virginia Community College System and accepted for credit by the state's four-year colleges (Virginia State Council of Higher Education and the Virginia State Department of Community Colleges, 1991). Both represent a recognition that many community college students who transfer do so without the associate's degree. A recent study of community college transfer students at randomly-selected universities in thirteen states revealed that only thirty-seven percent attained associate's degrees before moving on to the university; the number of semester-hour credits earned by the students before transferring ranged from one to over 100 (Palmer, Ludwig, and Stapleton, 1994).

At issue in discussions of prescription is the role of the community college in baccalaureate education. Because community college students may transfer without completing an associate's degree, the act of transfer itself does not necessarily signify that the student has met a specific standard of achievement. Although there are variations among states and disciplines, on the whole the community college contribution to undergraduate education varies from student to student. On the one hand, this reflects the role of the community college as an institution of convenience, offering courses that students may take as they see fit to meet idiosyncratic ends. The cost of this convenience, though, may be wariness on the part of receiving four-year colleges that remain unsure of the qualifications of those community college students who come knocking at their doors.

Curriculum Content

Though the components of the formal curriculum have remained stable over time, the content of the curriculum has not. Ways of knowing and the knowledge bases within disciplines are constantly being challenged. And because undergraduate education serves as a capstone period of schooling for individuals who do not pursue postgraduate study, assumptions about the ends of general education and about the relative merits of the pedagogical methods used to pursue those ends also come into play. Without substantive deliberations between institutions, the undergraduate offerings at two-year and four-year colleges may diverge considerably despite an outwardly similar curriculum structure. Even if they do not, a perception of differences, especially on the part of receiving four-year colleges, may thrive in the absence of first-hand knowledge gained through ongoing faculty discussions. University faculty and their departments have been known to go their own way, bypassing articulation agreements to impose their own transfer criteria when the product of the community college is distrusted (see, for example, Bowles, 1988). Upper-division general education requirements constitute a predominant example.

Deliberations about content take several forms. Some are the product of state initiatives; the faculty deliberations that led to the Illinois general education sequence (discussed above), for example. Others represent the occasional attempts of two-year and four-year college educators to speak with one voice about expectations concerning the skills of entering students. For example, the academic senates of the California Community Colleges, California State University, and the University of California have outlined English and mathematics competencies expected of high school graduates upon matriculation as freshmen (Academic Senates, 1982). Disciplinary organizations have also played a role. In Illinois, for example, two-year and four-year college faculty belonging to the Illinois Speech and Theatre Association met during the 1980s "to define the outcomes expected of the general education speech communication course required by most colleges and universities and, then, to define the appropriate content for the lower division courses in . . . various speech majors" (Illinois Board of Higher Education, 1992, p. 18). Finally, faculty from individual four-year and two-year colleges sometimes meet to discuss specific problems (such as a difference of opinion concerning the programming language to use in introductory computer science courses) or to examine more intangible matters, as in the case of teachers of Spanish examining the meaning and measurement of foreign language proficiency (Gill, 1992; Grossbach, 1991).

The impacts of these deliberations have not been assessed. To date, the literature yields more description than analysis. An intangible benefit appears to be the intellectual stimulus derived from the opportunity to converse with colleagues about the usually private world of teaching. Faculty members who have engaged in these deliberations often comment on this phenomenon. Reflecting on his work in convening faculty from the Community College of Philadelphia with faculty from two receiving institutions, Grossbach (1991, p. 7) notes that "most [participants] had not had an opportunity to talk with faculty from other colleges in any sustained way. In fact, the seminar provided an opportunity for some faculty from the same school to meet one another!" He goes on to note that attending each of the faculty meetings was one of the most intellectually stimulating things he had done in years. This bespeaks the characteristic isolation of undergraduate teaching and suggests that many faculty members would welcome an opportunity to think aloud with colleagues about the work of classroom teaching.

More concrete results may also emerge. In some cases, for example, curricula are aligned in small but important ways. The Borough of Manhattan Community College worked with a receiving institution to develop a joint six-credit mathematics sequence for students majoring in elementary education (Eaton, 1992). Sometimes, common teaching methodologies are explored. Faculty at the Houston Community Colleges and the University of Houston developed joint curriculum teams in English, mathematics, and history. These teams "met on a monthly basis to develop [instructional] goals . . . , to prepare instruction based on these goals, and to decide on classroom research techniques that could be used to assess their effectiveness" (Eaton, 1992, p. 36).

In other cases, ambiguities and hidden barriers in course-by-course articulation agreements are clarified or exposed. An illustration comes from Montclair State College (New Jersey), where department chairs have reviewed curricula at sending community colleges in order to identify those courses that should be accepted for credit. This college-wide approach to articulation, which involved discussions with faculty and chairs at the two-year colleges, was undertaken in response to the fear that transfer bridges offered by institutional articulation agreements may be illusory if disciplinary requisites are not recognized. "It is entirely possible, for instance, for a mathematics course at a two-year college to be equivalent to a corresponding mathematics course at a four-year institution and yet be unacceptable in fulfilling the designated mathematics requirement of a particular program" (Weinman and Dutka, 1993, p. 39).

These are modest gains that bespeak the nascent character of faculty deliberations between two-year and four-year colleges. A more substantial goal rarely achieved within institutions, let alone between them, might be a set of principles delineating purpose and method in undergraduate education—either as a whole or within specific disciplines. Such principles might draw on the work of disciplinary organizations. For example, a joint task force of the Mathematical Association of America and the Association of American Colleges has offered a set of goals and principles for undergraduate mathematics (Steen and others, 1990). Or they might draw on proposed structures for general education, such as the "utopian" general education model proposed by Arthur Cohen and Florence Brawer. Under this model, general education within the college is administered by a separate academic department whose faculty devote themselves solely to general education and who become experts in conceptualizing disciplinary knowledge in ways that make it useful to nonspecialists (Cohen and Brawer, 1989). The model may be too radical for full implementation, but it at least offers a way of conceptualizing general education and thinking about the weaknesses of most general education programs, which are administrative orphans within the academy.

Other illustrative, albeit not strictly replicable, models for educational guidelines can be found at the K–12 level. The Report of the Committee of Ten on Secondary Schools (1893) is the most famous; it delineated a structure for secondary education that endures to a large extent today. More recently, educators that belong to the Coalition of Essential Schools have sought to structure the high school experience around nine principles that emphasize students' abilities to perform complex cognitive tasks rather than to regurgitate facts. The interesting aspect of these principles is that they are guidelines for action—for structuring the work of the school—and not simply restatements of ideals. The first principle, which is strikingly similar to Eaton's (1994) call for a reaffirmation of the collegiate function at community colleges, states that high schools "should not attempt to be 'comprehensive' if such a claim is made at the expense of the school's central intellectual focus" (Sizer, 1986, p. 41). Principle nine ties this focus to the budget, noting that services often provided to students in comprehensive schools may have to be reduced or eliminated in order to keep the pupil-teacher ratio at a level that will sustain rigorous teaching (Sizer, 1986, p. 41).

Principles such as these are not ends unto themselves; they are what educators make of them and can too easily become platitudes that mask inaction. A notable limitation lies in their tendency to focus on process rather than outcomes. Nonetheless, they have the potential to expand the common language of faculty deliberations, adding to the shared understandings about curriculum structure a shared understanding about the purpose of undergraduate education.

Faculty Roles

Clearly, any joint principles developed by two-year and four-year colleges would have to consider faculty work, for a key assumption of the academic approach—and of pronouncements generally about the reform of undergraduate education—is that faculty members from the two-year and four-year sectors will *attend* to the undergraduate curriculum, not simply teach courses. They need to view themselves not only as disciplinary experts, but as pedagogical experts who build and evaluate curricula, determining the ends and means of undergraduate study. They also need to view themselves as colleagues in a shared enterprise.

Realization of these ideals will require educators at both four-year and two-year colleges to reconsider the traditional isolation of the classroom teacher. The lingering reality of teaching as a private and idiosyncratic task rather than as a technology that can be studied and discussed offers a haphazard framework for deliberations. Despite ongoing attempts to improve undergraduate teaching, it still lacks—on the whole—what Rau and Baker (1989, p. 166) call "the publicly validated system of technical expertise and evaluation found in research." In contrast to research, which is guided by studied methodology, consultation with colleagues, and rigorous peer review, teaching is often conducted alone, guided only by one's experience and by the occasional advice of others (Baker, 1986). Without a shared technical vocabulary, faculty members in both the two-year and four-year sectors are individual artisans, not a community of professionals who collectively study teaching and learning at the undergraduate level. The sense of shared understanding that facilitates discussions of the formal undergraduate curriculum is more difficult to achieve in discussions of what and how to teach.

Faculty in both sectors will also have to reconsider their disciplinary work. For example, interviews with some four-year college faculty participating in NCAAT projects reveal that reward structures emphasizing research and publication discouraged professors (especially those without tenure) from investing their energies in curriculum development activities (Callan and Reeves, 1994). Until teaching and curriculum development are considered legitimate scholarly contributions within disciplines, as suggested by Boyer (1990), this reluctance will be hard to overcome. Its alleged affects on the quality of undergraduate education have long been deplored. Eble (1990) has harshly commented on what he sees as the "degradation" of undergraduate education at four-year institutions.

As for the two-year institution, a tradition of faculty detachment from disciplinary communities will have to be questioned. The academic model of articulation runs counter to the long-held belief that strong ties to the discipline discourage attention to the institutional focus of the community college: students and their development. The deprecation of disciplinary ties, a consistent theme in the writing of many junior and community college leaders (Palmer, 1992), has most recently been voiced by Baker, Roueche, and Gillett-Karam (1990), who assert, "A major challenge for the leadership of community colleges is to cause the faculty members to see themselves first as members of the college community and secondly as members of their specific professional community" (p. 291). This viewpoint obviously distances the community college from academe, perpetuates four-year college skepticism of the two-year college enterprise, and causes those working on articulation to fall back on interinstitutional agreements rather than on collegial work toward shared ends.

The picture of universities as hostile environments for the lower division and of the community college as an adisciplinary and insular institution should not be overblown. It is too easy to resort to stereotype, ignoring the many exceptions in which faculty have excelled as undergraduate educators. Nonetheless, faculty need to determine how their accustomed roles help work toward or mitigate against their full participation in the work of constructing and assessing undergraduate curricula.

Conclusion: The Radical Implications of the Practical

Deliberations about the structure of the curriculum, about the content of courses, and about faculty roles have the potential to offer a cohesive undergraduate experience for the many students who use community colleges on the way to the bachelor's degree. Facilitating these deliberations also recognizes the fact that what faculty do in one sector affects the work of faculty in the other. Clearly, community college instructors must recognize the requisites of entry into upper-division courses and teach accordingly. And as Grossbach (1991, p. 7) has explained, four-year college faculty have an interest in the courses taught by two-year college faculty not only because they affect the skill levels of students, but also because what happens in introductory courses in a particular discipline often determines whether students will ever take another course in that discipline.

But however practical, the view of articulation as a function of faculty work in shaping undergraduate education is radical, for it ties articulation to what Meyer, Scott, and Deal (1981) call the institution's "core technology"—faculty teaching. The academic approach challenges education's long history of shielding this institutional core from potentially disturbing demands emanating outside the college or school. Rather than leaving the faculty undisturbed in their classrooms through reliance on student services and articulation agreements, the academic approach asks faculty to make transfer and articulation part of their responsibility for determining purpose and method in undergraduate education.

As such, the academic approach to articulation joins a host of other reforms whose proponents are struggling to involve faculty as key players. Tinto (1993), for example, has called for increased faculty involvement in colleges' efforts to improve student retention; but these efforts, as he notes, are usually the responsibility of student services personnel. The so-called *outcomes assessment movement* offers another example. Its proponents see faculty involvement as highly desirable and suggest that at a minimum the task of formulating institutional goals and objectives for learning will spur faculty interest in talking about and improving their teaching (Banta, 1991). But the formulation of tests used to assess the effects of the curriculum as a whole (as opposed to tests used to sort students in the classroom) is often led by outside professional test makers, such as the American College Testing Program (Palmer, 1993, pp. 52–53). The outcomes assessment movement has not yet been able to buck the entrenched American tradition of separating test development from curriculum development. Hence the teacher in his or her classroom remains relatively undisturbed.

The curious separation of the work of faculty from larger efforts to build and assess the curriculum poses a challenge to almost all reform efforts, transfer included. In the end, it becomes easier to talk about reform in the abstract or to build edifices on the periphery of the academy that demonstrate institutional concern with and effort in the effect of desired changes. Meyer, Scott, and Deal (1981, p. 156) have noted this tendency in the schools, arguing that their "organizational structures are decoupled from the technical work of education and many of its vagaries and problems." But there is nonetheless enough evidence that at least some faculty members are dismayed by this isolation and would welcome a chance to shape the programs that their students go through. The work of these faculty members should be studied and encouraged.

References

Academic Senates of the California Community Colleges, the California State University, and the University of California. *Statements on Preparation in English and Mathematics: Competencies Expected of Entering Freshmen and Remedial and Baccalaureate-Level Course Work.* Unpublished paper, 1982. (ED 222 235)

Baker, G. A., III, Roueche, J. E., and Gillett-Karam. *Teaching as Leading: Profiles of Excellence in the Open-Door College.* Washington, D.C.: American Association of Community and Junior Colleges, 1990.

Baker, P. J. "The Helter-Skelter Relationship Between Teaching and Research: A Cluster of Problems and Small Wins." *Teaching Sociology,* 1986, *14,* 50–66.

Banta, T. W. "Faculty-Developed Approaches to Assessing General Education Outcomes." *Assessment Update,* 1991, 3 (2), 1–2, 4.

Belcher, M., and Baldwin, A. *The Community College and Transfer: Some Indicators from State Data.* Miami, Fla.: Miami-Dade Community College, 1991. (ED 331 556)

Bowles, D. "Enhancing Articulation and Transfer." In C. Prager (ed.), *Enhancing Articulation and Transfer.* New Directions for Community Colleges, no. 61. San Francisco: Jossey-Bass, 1988.

Boyer, E. L. *Scholarship Reconsidered: Priorities of the Professoriate.* Princeton, N.J.: Carnegie Foundation for the Advancement of Teaching, 1990. (ED 326 149)

Callan, P. M., and Reeves, K. *Lessons Learned from the National Center for Academic Achievement and Transfer.* San Jose, Calif.: California Higher Education Policy Center, 1994.

Cohen, A. M., and Brawer, F. B. *The American Community College.* San Francisco: Jossey-Bass, 1989.

Committee of Ten on Secondary School Studies. *Report of the Committee on Secondary School Studies Appointed at the Meeting of the National Education Association July 9, 1892.* Washington, D.C.: Government Printing Office, 1893.

Eaton, J. S. *The Academic Model of Transfer.* Washington, D.C.: National Center for Academic Achievement and Transfer, 1990.

Eaton, J. S. *Faculty and Transfer: Academic Partnerships at Work.* Washington, D.C.: American Council on Education, 1992. (ED 344 630)

Eaton, J. S. *Strengthening Collegiate Education in Community Colleges.* San Francisco: Jossey-Bass, 1994.

Eble, K. "The Degradation of Undergraduate Education." In F. Jussawalla (ed.), *Excellent Teaching in a Changing Academy: Essays in Honor of Kenneth E. Eble.* New Directions for Teaching and Learning, no. 44. San Francisco: Jossey-Bass, 1990.

Gill, R. K. *Articulating Programs Between Two- and Four-Year Institutions by Identifying Course and Program Competencies.* Unpublished doctoral project completed in partial fulfillment of the doctor of arts degree, George Mason University, 1992. (ED 354 026)

Grossbach, B. L. "Generating Faculty Dialogue Across Colleges: A Personal Experience." *Transfer Working Papers,* 1991, 2 (1). (ED 327 245)

Illinois Board of Higher Education. *Undergraduate Education: Transfer and Articulation.* Springfield: IBHE, 1992. (ED 343 638)

Illinois Board of Higher Education. *The Illinois Articulation Initiative: The General Education Core Curriculum.* Springfield: IBHE, 1994. (ED 371 785)

Kimball, B. A. "The Historical and Cultural Dimensions of the Recent Reports on Undergraduate Education. In C. F. Conrad and J. G. Haworth (eds.), *Curriculum in Transition: Perspectives on the Undergraduate Experience,* Needham Heights, Mass.: Ginn Press, 1990.

Knoell, D. "Improving Transfer Effectiveness." In G. A. Baker III (ed.), *A Handbook on the Community College in America: Its History, Mission, and Management,* Westport, Conn.: Greenwood Press, 1994.

Meyer, J. W., Scott, W. R., and Deal, T. E. "Institutional and Technical Sources of Organizational Structure: Explaining the Structure of Educational Organizations." In H. D. Stein (ed.), *Organization and the Human Services,* Philadelphia: Temple University Press, 1981.

Najee-ullah, D., and others. *Minorities in Mathematics: Georgia State University–Atlanta Metropolitan College Partnership Project. Final Report.* Atlanta: Atlanta Metropolitan College, 1993. (ED 368 550)

Palmer, J. C. "Faculty Professionalism Reconsidered." In K. Kroll (ed.), *Maintaining Faculty Excellence.* New Directions for Community Colleges, no. 79. San Francisco: Jossey-Bass, 1992.

Palmer, J. C. "Institutional Accreditation, Student Outcomes Assessment, and the Open-Ended Institution." In C. Prager (ed.), *Accreditation of the Two-Year College.* New Directions for Community Colleges, no. 83. San Francisco: Jossey-Bass, 1993.

Palmer, J. C., and Eaton, J. S. "Building the National Agenda for Transfer: A Background Paper." In *Setting the National Agenda: Academic Achievement and Transfer.* Washington, D.C.: American Council on Education, 1991.

Palmer, J. C., Ludwig, M., and Stapleton, L. *At What Point Do Community College Students Transfer to Baccalaureate-Granting Institutions? Evidence from a 13-State Study.* Washington, D.C.: American Council on Education, 1994. (ED 373 844)

Rau, W., and Baker, P. J. (1989). "The Organized Contradictions of Academe: Barriers Facing the Next Academic Revolution." *Teaching Sociology,* 1994, *17,* 161–175.

Sizer, T. R. "Rebuilding: First Steps by the Coalition of Essential Schools. *Phi Delta Kappan,* 1986, *68* (1), 38–42.

Steen, L. A., and others. *Challenges for College Mathematics: An Agenda for the Next Decade. Report of a Joint Task Force.* Washington, D.C.: Association of American Colleges, Mathematical Association of America, 1990. (ED 367 529)

Tinto, V. *Leaving College.* Chicago: University of Chicago Press, 1993.

Veysey, L. (1990). "Stability and Experiment in the American Undergraduate Curriculum." In C. F. Conrad and J. G. Haworth (eds.), *Curriculum in Transition: Perspectives on the Undergraduate Experience.* Needham Heights, Mass.: Ginn Press, 1990.

Virginia State Council of Higher Education and the Virginia State Department of Community Colleges. *State Policy on Transfer.* Richmond: VSCHE and VSDCC, 1991. (ED 339 441)

Weinman, E., and Dutka, J. T. "Transfer and Articulation: Using a Team Approach." *College and University,* 1993, *69* (1), 38–42.

JAMES C. PALMER is associate professor of educational administration and foundations at Illinois State University.

*This chapter discusses the underlying implications of transfer and
articulation policy on the activities that take place at the local level—
the individual community college.*

Transfer and Articulation Policies:
Implications for Practice

Tronie Rifkin

Since the early philosophical discourse on the community college movement,
transfer and articulation practices in community colleges have expanded into
a complex enterprise involving national organizations, legislators, federal agencies, accrediting bodies, state agencies, and administrators and faculty from all
education sectors. The overall community college effort dedicated to transfer
and articulation, however, has waxed and waned over the years because of
struggles over the community college's purpose as an institution. Because community colleges are multifunctional institutions, there are constant tensions
between the community college as an educational center, occupational institution, or liberal arts and transfer institution (Eaton, 1994). Yet, the transfer
function has remained critical because of its role in the realization of equal
opportunity in American higher education. Despite the apparent commitment
to transfer education, current conditions within the higher education environment are challenging existing policies and practices. These conditions are:
declining enrollment coupled with economic recessions at the state and
national levels; significant changes in the composition of the student body with
regard to age, ethnicity, socioeconomic status, and academic and career orientations; increasing competition among public agencies for limited state
resources; major shifts in the priorities of public policy from access to achievement; and the increasing vocationalization of both community colleges and
baccalaureate-granting institutions (Ahumada, 1993; Barkley, 1993).

The chapters in this volume have presented current transfer and articulation policies and practices as well as the influences of the changing environmental conditions under which they operate. The purpose of this chapter is to
identify trends from the preceding chapters and to discuss the underlying

implications for practice of policies that are intended to maintain a viable community college transfer function that will better serve the institution's educational goals and the educational goals of this nation into the twenty-first century.

Role of History

In order to understand a phenomenon more fully, one must understand its historical context. Kintzer's (Chapter One) historiography reveals the development, emergence, and growth of transfer and articulation policies and practices from the beginning of the nineteenth century through the 1980s. Over the decades, transfer and articulation practices have adopted different patterns and directions among community colleges and between states. By the 1980s, several articulation and transfer issues emerged as central to assessing the future of community colleges.

One such issue is the expanding role of the state in developing transfer and articulation policies. In what ways are states becoming more involved? What are the areas in which the states are involved and how does that involvement impact existing transfer and articulation practices? Though the role of the state is ever more present, how the mandates and legislation are translated at the community college level may very well depend on the culture of the particular community college and the interests and attitudes of its constituents. For example, the needs of a small rural community college may be quite different from the needs of an urban community college.

Second, the transfer rate is important as a measure of how many students pass through two-year colleges on their way to baccalaureate institutions. For most of the 1980s, few community colleges had the technological capability to collect valid and reliable student data. Transfer rates were not reported with any precision or consistency across states or institutions. Today, many institutions can collect relevant information on students and maintain databases that can provide reliable information on transfer students and their enrollment patterns. Despite the greater amount of data available, there is a lack of any systematic means of assessing institutional transfer rates. As a result, it is difficult to determine whether past problems of access and articulation have been solved, whether changes have occurred in the demographics and related interests of community college students that have led to an increased emphasis on occupational education over transfer, or whether the institution has been effective in implementing its transfer mission.

A third issue concerns the changing student population and equal access for underrepresented groups. The transfer student population is changing to include not just recent high school graduates, but vocational and technical students and adult learners as well. In addition, efforts to improve minority access to community colleges began with programs like The Ford Foundation Urban Community Colleges Transfer Opportunity Program (UCCTOP). Currently, these efforts are threatened by the current political climate opposing affirmative action. Thus, the question is, How can transfer and articulation processes accommodate the changing student population and a greater representation of minority students? Another consideration is how to improve the articulation process so that students can experience a cohesive undergraduate education, including not having to repeat courses. Suggestions include curriculum deliberations involving faculty and collaboration between community colleges and their four-year transfer institutions. Public accountability for higher education combined with reduced funding levels has made it imperative that community colleges and four-year institutions communicate, collaborate, and cooperate in the delivery of higher education.

State Influence Versus Local Community College Activities

The influence of the state is an important aspect of the transfer and articulation process. In 1985, Kintzer and Wattenbarger asserted that more formalized state articulation and transfer policies assure better transfer opportunities for students statewide. Today, Robertson and Frier (Chapter Two) suggest that the purpose of state involvement is not only to assure better transfer opportunities for students but to improve the quality of education by coordinating the resources and participation of the entire community and each sector of the education system.

Palmer and Eaton (1991), in their policy statement on transfer education, assert that quality in higher education is determined by the extent to which students moving from two-year to four-year schools are prepared to meet the collegiate expectations of the four-year institutions, the ease with which students are able to move from one institution to another, and the rate of baccalaureate degree attainment among transfer students compared to that among students native to the four-year institutions (p. 4). Clearly defined admissions standards, including standardized assessment that reflect the educational requirements and qualifications expected of its students, are devices with which some states begin the process of ensuring that students are prepared to progress toward the baccalaureate degree. Also, mandates to centralize information concerning student transfer such as student progress, course prerequisites, and transferability of courses are designed to improve student flow from high school to community college to public four-year institutions in the state. The push by states for community colleges to make use of available technology and construct large information databases on students will provide institutions with a means of determining the rate at which students transfer successfully. In these respects state influence can facilitate transfer. Other research on facilitating transfer has recommended and even encouraged state involvement. For example, Banks (1994), in a study of the environmental influences on transfer, recommended pressure from the state to establish a set of core courses within community colleges that would transfer to local institutions in order to improve transfer activity at some community colleges. She also suggested that state initiatives can offset negative environmental conditions that affect transfer such as local unemployment and community income.

Though states are taking a more active role in the community college transfer function, the locus of transfer and articulation activities take place at the local level—the individual community college. As Cohen's comparative policy study of high and low transfer rate colleges reveals, "transfer is a function of college activities and the perceptions held by students and staff members" (Chapter Three). The differences between high- and low-transfer colleges was evident in the degree to which the particular community college emphasized transfer as an academic objective through transfer assistance programs and services such as transfer centers, faculty and staff participation in developing transfer programs and services, academic visibility and interaction of faculty with students, and an attitude among administrators that transfer is one of the top priorities of the institution. Thus, although states mandate definite admissions policies, course equivalencies, implementation of technology in order to centralize information, and collaboration between all sectors of the education system, ultimately the future effectiveness of transfer is the degree to which the individual community colleges view transfer as an academic objective. Even though financial incentives and accountability measures may encourage institutions to promote transfer, if the responsibility and authority within an institution is not so directed and motivated, the impact is likely to be minimal. However, it should be noted that the emphasis on transfer should not be at the expense of other educational missions of the community college. The point is more that state involvement can help facilitate transfer success, whereas the desired outcome can only be achieved by the community college and its members.

Transfer Rates—A Measure of Success?

While states can facilitate transfer by legislating certain program and policy changes, how will the success of these changes be measured? Transfer activity is measured by a transfer rate. The problem is that there are several different definitions of *transfer rate* and the formula used to calculate it. As is evident from Spicer and Armstrong's chapter, the issue is over the definition of the potential pool of transfer students, or, in other words, the denominator in the transfer rate formula.

As Laanan and Sanchez point out, there are the traditional transfer rate models that consider the eligible pool of transfer students to consist of all first-time college students who have earned some combination of credits within a specified period of time (Cohen, 1991; Berman, Weiler, and Associates, 1990; McMillan and Parke, 1994). There also are emerging alternative models. The results of a study assessing transfer activity in community colleges across the nation conducted by the American Association of Community Colleges (AACC) and the National Center for Academic Achievement and Transfer acknowledged that transfer rate and transfer effectiveness are separate issues

(1992). The study defines effectiveness by comparing the number of students who do transfer to those who intended to transfer when they entered college. Following the AACC study, several other educators have attempted to specify alternative ways of measuring transfer activity that differentiate between different transfer types and that consider transfer eligibility or readiness as a key factor in the definition (Boese and Birdsall, 1994; Rasor and Barr, 1995; Baratta, 1992). Laanan and Sanchez argue that these alternative transfer definitions measure different forms of transfer effectiveness that may provide a better indicator of the community college's contribution to higher education.

Spicer and Armstrong demonstrate how both traditional and nontraditional transfer rate formulas produce quite a wide range of outcomes, all dependent on how the pool of eligible transfer students is defined. This demonstration simply returns us to the original question. What is a reliable and relevant measure of transfer success? As mentioned by the authors of both Chapters Four and Five, each model has its own strengths and weaknesses. Perhaps the goal should not be to determine one standard measure of transfer but to determine which measure of transfer should be used when and for what purpose. In their conclusion, Spicer and Armstrong suggest that transfer rates, like other educational indicators, "are difficult to use both as a program accountability tool for external audiences, and for local planning and program review purposes" (Chapter Five). Hirose (1994) has also argued that once colleges calculate and report their standard transfer rate, campuses can use their own data "to modify the definition and examine their own categories of students by examining factors such as student aspirations, gender, ethnicity, age, socioeconomic status, disabilities, courses taken, and participation in special activities" (p. 68). Similarly, Palmer and Eaton (1991) have suggested variables to include in testing hypotheses about transfer rates: strength of the liberal arts curriculum, transfer arrangements with four-year colleges, and matriculation and guidance practices. Because it can be said that no two community colleges are alike, and because of the diversity in the academic background, educational goals, and enrollment patterns of community college students, it seems that one transfer rate may not provide the most complete picture of the transfer activity at any given community college (Laanan and Sanchez, Chapter Four). Therefore, rather than arguing about which transfer rate to adopt as the standard, state policy makers, higher education officials, and local community college leaders need to review the various transfer definitions and formulas and determine which rates are acceptable for national and state program accountability purposes and which represent the community college's effectiveness in preparing students for transfer.

Articulation and the Changing Student Population

Community college students who declare an interest in transferring to four-year institutions are quite different from the high school graduates who enrolled in community colleges thirty years ago. Today, potential transfer students, according to Knoell, include the "unemployed, displaced workers, and those in need of upgrading employment skills; welfare recipients; women reentering higher education after a hiatus; and 'interrupted scholars' with diverse interests, objectives, and educational backgrounds" (Chapter Six). Barkley (1993) notes the phenomenon of *swirling* as another change in the transfer student population—those students who attend one or more colleges during their enrollment at a particular community college. Grubb (1991) also asserts that many students who pursue transfer are as likely to have vocational or technical degrees as academic degrees. As the student population grows more diverse in academic backgrounds, educational goals, enrollment patterns, and socioeconomic status and ethnic heritage, colleges are faced with student tracking challenges, coordination of programs, and articulation of individual courses.

Knoell argues that community colleges need to recognize the variety in their student bodies and seek new opportunities for them such as expanding course offerings beyond the two-year associate's degree, prepare graduates to become faculty and staff in high schools and two-year institutions, and place new emphasis on high school-through-community college tech-prep programs, among others (see Chapter Six). The way these new transfer opportunities can be achieved is by implementing a collaborative model of articulation that does not follow the traditional faculty and staff review of community college courses and programs in order to make judgments about their transferability to a four-year institution. Knoell proposes evaluation of student portfolios that include work and life experience, joint admissions to both a community college and a four-year institution with transfer guaranteed to those who successfully fulfill certain predetermined criteria, agreed-upon assessment instruments and standards for determining transfer eligibility, joint use of facilities, opportunities for high school juniors and seniors to earn college credit, joint professional development opportunities for two-year and four-year faculty, joint development of courses, and two-year and four-year faculty cooperation in establishing general education requirements. Because collaborative efforts of this nature are labor-intensive and require commitment to the process from faculty, staff, and students, community colleges are not expected to consider all of these approaches. However, it is imperative that they explore the possibilities of implementing one or more.

There are many reasons for institutions to initiate cooperative arrangements. Some arrangements are motivated by distance considerations, others grow from historic and demographic connections between the two-year and four-year institutions, and others are constructed for economic or political reasons. In this volume, Palmer (Chapter Seven) raises another reason: to encourage faculty participation in and responsibility for determining form and content in the curriculum, thereby generating discussion about the purpose and method of undergraduate education. Interinstitutional faculty involvement in determining the course sequences, format, and content is particularly critical today when the need to educate, train, and provide advanced education for an increasingly technical work force is growing. With this growth will come an increased need to articulate the technical and vocational programs at the bac-calaureate level and to design programs that build upon the applied science degree (Prager, 1988; Barkley, 1993). The framework for a discussion of the technical or career student transfer phenomenon has not been positive. Typi-cally, the debate centers on a concern that any vocational emphasis is likely to lead to a decrease in a liberal arts and science emphasis and a subsequent decrease in critical thinking skills. However, Cohen and Brawer (1989) main-tain that the pursuit of career curricula may have greater intrinsic value than has been considered. It may cultivate an interest in career mobility and in turn stimulate student aspirations beyond the associate's degree.

Given the diversity in the academic and career aspirations of the commu-nity college student, interinstitutional faculty deliberations surrounding the cur-riculum are key to the implementation and eventual success of any of the approaches to articulation described by Knoell (Chapter Six). In addition, as both Knoell and Palmer maintain, collaboration is an essential element to any articu-lation effort whether it takes place at the community college or the state level.

Conclusion

Drawing implications and foretelling the future of transfer and articulation pol-icy from history and current state and institutional practices are not easy tasks. However, some elements appear more pervasive than others. Clearly, there is a growing interest in facilitating the transfer and articulation process from the state through initiatives concerning admissions standards, course equivalen-cies, database building, and financial incentives. State interests are also evident in policy debates over what is a meaningful measure of student transfer, and state influence is reflected in articulation practices. Although the transfer and articulation process is a state concern as well as a national issue, the actual real-ization of policy initiatives always takes place at the local community college level. Evident throughout the chapters in this volume, what takes place at the institutional level is ultimately what determines the effectiveness of transfer and articulation practices. Cohen's study (Chapter Three), in particular, shows how the community college culture is exemplified by an institution-wide emphasis on transfer through programs and services, and administrator, fac-ulty, and staff interest and involvement in creating this culture. Also, decisions regarding which transfer rate to use that best describes the individual com-munity college's contribution to transfer can only be arrived at by the mem-bers of the institution. Likewise, when it comes to implementing collaborative models of articulation, the discussions over curriculum content, educational purpose and methods, course prerequisites, and transferability of courses will inevitably take place at the institutional level, even if the discussions are directed by state mandate. It is, thus, probable that transfer and articulation policies and practices will continue to represent a struggle between state demands for public accountability and serving the academic and career aspi-rations of community college students.

Since the 1900s, transfer and articulation have evolved into a complex system. Over the decades, progress has been made to improve the process within individual community colleges, between education sectors, and within and between states; and improvements to make the transfer function more effective will continue as long as community colleges are willing to confront, grapple with, and manage these issues. As Kintzer states in Chapter One, "I continue to stress the importance of attitude—commitment to the total process. . . . As responsibility for developing articulation and transfer policies continues to expand into political arenas involving many types of quasieducational institutions and organizations, a positive attitude and willingness to collaborate remains critically important." The authors of this volume have presented recommendations for current and future transfer and articulation policies in an attempt to expand the discourse and thereby enhance the ability of community colleges to meet their many goals.

References

Ahumada, M. M. "Inter-Institutional Articulation and Transfer: The Role of Data Bases and Information Systems." *Community College Journal of Research and Practice,* 1993, *17,* 141–152.

American Association of Community Colleges. *Policy Statement on Institutional Effectiveness.* Washington, D.C.: American Association of Community Colleges, 1992.

Banks, D. L. "Effects of Environmental Conditions on Student-Transfer Activity." *Community College Journal of Research and Practice,* 1994, *18* (3), 245–259.

Barkley, S. M. "A Synthesis of Recent Literature on Articulation and Transfer." *Community College Review,* 1993, *20* (4), 39–50.

Baratta, F. "Profile of District Transfers to the University of California, California State University, and St. Mary's College." Martinez, Calif.: Contra Costa Community College District, Office of District Research, 1992. (ED 920 457)

Berman, P., Weiler, D., and Associates. *Enhancing Transfer Effectiveness: A Model for the 1990s.* Washington, D.C.: American Association of Community and Junior Colleges, 1990. (ED 324 050)

Boese, L. and Birdsall, L. "Measuring Transfer Eligibility: Definitions, Procedures, and Initial Findings." Paper presented at the California Association of Institutional Research, Annual Conference, San Diego, November 1994.

Cohen, A. M. *A Model for Deriving the Transfer Rate: Report of the Transfer Assembly Project.* Washington, D.C.: American Association of Community Colleges, 1991.

Cohen, A. M., and Brawer, F. B. *The American Community College.* San Francisco: Jossey-Bass, 1989.

Eaton, J. S. *Strengthening Collegiate Education in Community Colleges.* San Francisco: Jossey-Bass, 1994.

Grubb, W. N. "The Decline of Community College Transfer Rates." *Journal of Higher Education,* 1991, *62,* 194–217.

Hirose, S. M. "Calculating Student Transfer Rates: The Transfer Assembly Project." *Community College Review,* 1994, *22* (1), 62–71.

Kintzer, F. C. and Wattenbarger, J. L. *The Articulation/ Transfer Phenomenon: Patterns and Directions.* Washington, D.C.: American Association of Community and Junior Colleges, 1985. (ED 257 539)

McMillan, V. K., and Parke, S. J. "Calculating Transfer Rates: Examining Two National Models in Illinois." *Community College Review,* 1994, *22* (2), 69–77.

Palmer, J. C. and Eaton, J. S. "Building the National Agenda for Transfer: A Background Paper." *Setting the National Agenda: Academic Achievement and Transfer.* Washington, D.C.: American Council on Education, 1991. (ED 336 138)

Prager, C. (ed.). *Enhancing Articulation and Transfer.* New Directions for Community Colleges, no. 61. San Francisco: Jossey-Bass, 1988.

Rasor, R. A., and Barr, J. E. "The Transfer Eligible Rate: Longitudinal Results of a Companion Measure to the Transfer Rate." Paper presented at the Research and Planning Group for the California Community Colleges 1995 Annual Conference, San Diego, March 1995.

TRONIE RIFKIN is publications coordinator at the ERIC Clearinghouse for Community Colleges and a doctoral candidate in higher education at the Graduate School of Education and Information Studies, University of California, Los Angeles.

Because of the unique mission of community colleges, transfer and articulation practices influence student success as well as the quality of education provided at those colleges.

Sources and Information: The Transfer Function and Community Colleges

Matthew Burstein

One of the central elements of the mission of community colleges is preparing students for upper-division-level course work at a four-year institution. This transfer function involves providing students with a level of education comparable to the first two years of education at four-year institutions as well as information about upper-division programs and an institutional atmosphere that supports college transfer students. In addition to the programs at individual colleges, interinstitutional cooperation, articulation agreements, and transfer programs designed to ease student transfer efforts are important elements of the process. In many ways, institutional programs and state-wide articulation agreements play as much of a role in the success of student transfer as the quality of the colleges' education.

The following publications reflect the current ERIC literature on transfer programs and articulation agreements. Most ERIC documents (publications with ED numbers) can be viewed on microfiche at over nine hundred libraries worldwide. In addition, most may be ordered on microfiche or on paper from the ERIC Document Reproduction Service (EDRS) by calling (800) 443-ERIC. Journal articles are not available from EDRS, but they can be acquired through regular library channels or purchased from the University Microfilm International Articles Clearinghouse at (800) 248–0360.

The Impact of Policy on Transfer

These articles all discuss how the programs and institutional climate impact the transfer rates of community college students.

Timmerman, L., and others. *Transfer Success Work Group Report.* Austin: Community Colleges and Technical Institutes Division of the Texas Higher Education Coordinating Board, Texas Association of Junior and Community College Instructional Administrators, 1995. (ED 381 212)

The Transfer Success Work Group was established by the Texas Higher Education Coordinating Board (THECB) and the Texas Association of Junior and Community College Instructional Administrators to investigate the effectiveness of the state's public community college transfer function and to make recommendations for improving transfer efficiency. The Work Group identified common barriers to transfer from national research and examined transfer outcomes for Texas public community colleges as of 1994. The work group also conducted a survey of seventy-five instructional administrators and student support personnel at fifty-three institutions in the state, revealing that although an effective system to track transfer students and outcomes was rated as the third most important factor in transfer success, it ranked twenty-seventh among factors actually in place. Finally, the work group developed fifteen recommendations for state community colleges and the THECB related to the need to track and follow-up on student goals, retention, progress, completion, and transfer and to promote increased cooperation between two- and four-year colleges.

Creech, J. D. *Helping Students Who Transfer from Two-Year to Four-Year Colleges.* Atlanta, Ga.: Southern Regional Education Board, 1995. (ED 379 015)

This report describes policies and practices that can help administrators, faculty, and states improve the rate of transfer between two- and four-year colleges. Sections of the report include, "Helping Students Who Transfer from Two-Year to Four-Year Colleges," focusing on the importance of transfer programs and opportunities in southern states; "How Do We Know if Transfer Policies and Practices Are Working?" describing ways of measuring transfer activity; "Who Attends Two-Year Colleges?" offering a profile of students at a typical public two-year college in the southern region; "What Do Two-Year College Students Study?" and "What Policies and Practices Are Likely to Help Students Transfer?" focusing on transfer admission policies, early access to accurate transfer information, transferability and applicability of credit, institutional agreements, statewide agreements, general education core courses, common courses and course-numbering systems, and credits from vocational and technical programs; and two examples of comprehensive statewide guidelines and practices in North Carolina and Florida. The final section summarizes steps to a successful approach to developing transfer policies and practices.

Richardson, R. C., Jr. "Faculty in the Transfer and Articulation Process: Silent Partners or Missing Link?" *Community College Review,* 1993, *21* (1), 41–47.

This article describes the ways in which the particular duties and orientations of two- and four-year college faculty tend to remove faculty from the transfer process. It suggests the importance of an increased faculty role in the transfer process through such means as faculty advising of students and increased two- and four-year faculty interaction.

Turner, C.S.V. "It Takes Two to Transfer: Relational Networks and Educational Outcomes." *Community College Review,* 1992, *19* (4), 27–33.

This article reviews literature describing the complexity and difficulty of two- to four-year college transfer. It describes a comparative study of the transfer process for Hispanic and white students in three California community colleges and discusses the impact of interinstitutional linkages and networks on articulation and transfer.

Ludwig, M. J., and Palmer, J. C. *Guiding Future Research on the Community College Transfer Function: Summary of a National Seminar (Washington, D.C., September 21–22, 1992).* Washington, D.C.: National Center for Academic Achievement and Transfer, American Council on Education, 1993. (ED 354 973)

In September 1992, a small group of experienced researchers met to identify areas of research and specific research hypotheses to guide further inquiry into transfer. Specifically, participants examined transfer as it relates to institutional mission, institutional organization, and access to education and identified various premises upon which hypotheses might be structured.

Ignash, J. "Curricular Trends in Community Colleges: Implications for Transfer." Paper presented at the annual research conference of the Research and Planning Group for California Community Colleges, Tahoe City, Mar. 3–5, 1993. (ED 354 050)

In 1991, the Center for the Study of Community Colleges (CSCC) in Los Angeles conducted the seventh in a series of studies of trends in liberal arts course offerings in community colleges nationwide. During 1992, CSCC developed a taxonomy for non–liberal arts courses, and completed a course section tally using the same 164 community colleges participating in the 1991 study. Findings were combined with results from CSCC's ongoing Transfer Assembly Project to examine a number of research questions including areas of change in the community college curriculum, the relationship between curricular emphases and transfer rate, the percentage of non–liberal arts courses that are transferable to four-year institutions, and the relationship between institutional characteristics (such as size and location) and curricular offerings. The study found that a total of 104,565 course sections were tallied, of which 45,360 (43.4 percent) were non–liberal arts courses; while course offerings in agriculture and engineering have shown considerable decreases between 1978 and

1991, English-as-a-second-language course sections have increased dramatically during this same period, representing over half of all foreign language enrollments in 1991; and in California, close to two-thirds of non–liberal arts courses are transferable to comprehensive state universities. A detailed breakdown of course offerings by discipline area, a description of the taxonomy used for the six liberal arts discipline areas and the ten non–liberal arts discipline areas, data tables, and references are included.

Cipres, E. L., and Parish, C. L. "Transfer and Articulation: Gaining Institutional Support and Developing Regional Relationships." Paper presented at the 2nd International Conference for Community College Chairs, Deans, and Other Instructional Leaders, Phoenix, Ariz., Feb. 17–20, 1993. (ED 354 031)

At Mount San Antonio College (MSAC) in Walnut, California, a full-time classified position of Articulation Specialist was created in 1989 to help the college's articulation officer establish the necessary articulation agreements for facilitating the transfer of MSAC students to four-year institutions. The MSAC Transfer Center, one of twenty state-funded pilot projects operated cooperatively with the University of California and California State University, provides resources and services to assist students in formulating their transfer goals and developing a plan to achieve them. The five external factors that have the greatest impact on a college's articulation and transfer efforts and that are generally beyond the control of the college are economics, student demographics (which affect allocations of outside funds), community involvement, the proximity of primary transfer institutions, and the financing structure and state policy. Internal factors which affect articulation and transfer efforts include college mission and goals, organizational structure, administrative environment, and district funding. Achieving and maintaining financial and administrative support are the greatest challenges facing a colleges' transfer and articulation efforts.

Gill, R. K. "Articulating Programs between Two- and Four-Year Institutions by Identifying Course and Program Competencies." Unpublished doctoral dissertation, George Mason University, 1992. (ED 354 026)

Copies of this paper are not available from EDRS, but copies may be obtained from University Microfilms, 300 North Zeeb Road, Ann Arbor, Mich., 48106; order number 92–22351).

Research indicates that program articulation between two- and four-year institutions begins when faculty at both levels identify and validate the competencies that students should have. A study was conducted to develop a model methodology for articulating a program of study between a two- and four-year institution by identifying and validating course and program competencies. The methodology involved the use of a case study, articulating a computer science program at Anne Arundel Community College in Maryland, with the first two years of the corresponding program at Towson State University (Maryland). Faculty from both institutions supplied course syllabi, tests, quizzes, final exams, lab and homework assignments, class handouts, textbooks, and other supplemental material for all courses in the two programs during the 1991–92 academic year. These materials were analyzed, and a separate competency list was developed for each program. Program-to-program comparisons revealed compatibility except for minor differences. Course-to-course comparisons revealed more significant differences. Resolution of the differences should permit development of an articulation agreement. A discussion of the rationale for negotiating articulation agreements, a methodology for resolving differing competency requirements, copies of the competency lists, data tables, references, and workshop evaluations are included.

Laden, B. V. "An Exploratory Examination of Organizational Factors Leading to Transfer of Hispanic Students: A Case Study. ASHE Annual Meeting Paper." Paper presented at the annual meeting of the Association for the Study of Higher Education, Minneapolis, Minn., Oct. 29–Nov. 3, 1992. (ED 352 922)

Hispanics represent the fastest growing ethnic group nationally, yet many Hispanics continue to be undereducated and underemployed. This paper discusses one community college's success in preparing and transferring Hispanic students to four-year institutions. The study examined a San Francisco Bay Area high-transfer community college, which was experiencing an increase in the enrollment of Hispanic students, to determine how its organizational practices were specifically addressing the transfer of this population. Data are provided that were gathered through interviews with college personnel involved in carrying out the transfer function as part of their responsibilities. Exploratory analysis and findings of the data are presented in terms of four organizational dimensions: commitment, structural context, role performance of staff, and role performance of students.

Terzian, A. L. *Good Practices in Transfer Education: A Report from Two- and Four-Year Colleges and Universities.* Washington, D.C.: National Center for Academic Achievement and Transfer, American Council on Education, 1991. (ED 344 640)

In 1991, a national survey was conducted of transfer practices at both two- and four-year institutions. The survey was sent for the second time to two-year public and private institutions ($n = 1,350$) and for the first time to four-year institutions ($n = 1,950$). The two-year college response rate was 39 percent in 1990 and 31 percent in 1991, and the response rate for four-year institutions was 32 percent. Transfer practices prevalent in both the 1990 and 1991 two-year college responses were written articulation agreements, transfer counselors, and course equivalency guides. In the 1991 survey, other strategies cited to help students transfer included an articulated core curriculum, guaranteed admissions to four-year institutions, transfer centers, and computerized course transfer information services. In general, four-year institutions relied on fewer academic and student service practices to support the transfer process than their two-year counterparts. The two main practices employed by four-year institutions were transfer counselors and advisers and written articulation agreements. Four-year institutions were far less likely than two-year colleges to involve faculty in academic practices such as two-year/four-year departmental collaboration (30 percent versus 49 percent), two-year/four-year faculty collaboration (18 percent versus 36 percent), and joint degree programs (16 percent versus 24 percent).

Banks, D. L. "The Impact of the Organizational Environment on the Community College Transfer Function." Paper presented at the annual conference of the American Educational Research Association, San Francisco, Apr. 20–24, 1992. (ED 344 632)

In 1992, a study was conducted to examine the relationship between a number of organizational criteria and the community college transfer function. Using a case study approach, six California community colleges, with either above average or below average transfer rates, were assessed in terms of adaptive capacity; organizational culture and climate; governance processes; institutional communication, commitment, and focus; curriculum; activities to promote transfer; and social networks. Data were gathered from administrators, faculty, counselors, and students by means of questionnaires, interviews, analyses of reports, and site visits. The study found that survey respondents at high-transfer colleges felt greater loyalty and commitment to their institutions than low-transfer colleges; student services, such as retention programs and services for at-risk students, were given equal attention at high- and low-transfer colleges; high-transfer colleges stressed liberal arts courses in their curricula, whereas low-transfer colleges stressed general education and vocational courses; high-transfer colleges were significantly more likely to stress innovation in curricula and programs; student outcomes were the result of institutional practices and staff commitment to improving transfer education; institutional leadership was key in initiating and managing change within the college; and participatory governance was central to building commitment among college staff and inspiring them to become involved in their institution.

Articulation Agreements and Programs

The following articles provide information about various articulation programs:

Illinois State Board of Higher Education. *Policies on Transfer and the General Education Core Curriculum.* Springfield: IBHE, 1994. (ED 373 854)

In January 1993, the Illinois State Board of Higher Education, the Illinois Community College Board, and the Transfer Coordinators of Illinois Colleges and Universities launched the state's Articulation Initiative to develop a model general education curriculum that would be accepted as students transfer between the state's colleges and universities. The resulting General Education Core Curriculum (GECC) is designed to ensure the full transferability of credits for students attaining the associate's degree, for students transferring from a college before attaining an associate's degree, and for students transferring between baccalaureate degree–granting institutions. The GECC consists of courses designed to introduce students to the breadth of knowledge and the different modes of inquiry of different academic disciplines, balancing requirements among the core arts and sciences disciplines, and closely mirrors typical lower-division general education requirements of Illinois baccalaureate granting institutions. The requirements include three courses in communications, including a two-course sequence in writing and one course in oral communications; one to two courses in mathematics; two natural science courses, including one life science and one physical science, one of which must be a laboratory course; three humanities and fine arts courses, with at least one course from each division; and three courses in social and behavioral sciences, with courses selected from at least two disciplines.

Rubi, D. C. *Survey on the Transferability of Associate's Degree to Four-Year Institutions.* Phoenix: Arizona State Board of Directors for Community Colleges, 1994. (ED 369 449)

In January 1994, the Arizona State Board of Directors for Community Colleges (ASBDCC) conducted a survey of state four-year systems nationwide to determine the existence of standards regarding the transferability of associate's degrees and associate's-degree students' academic standing at receiving four-year institutions. Questionnaires were mailed to the four-year systems in forty-nine states, with responses being received from forty-one systems. The survey found that twenty-two of the responding states indicated that they had an arrangement or policy allowing for the transfer of the associate's degree. Of these states, thirteen indicated that the standards were mandated by state boards, four indicated that they were mandated by the legislature, and five indicated that they were voluntary. Of the forty-one responding states, seven indicated that the associate's degree satisfied general studies requirements, while nineteen stated that it lead to some form of junior class standing at the four-year institution. Also, the survey found that responses varied widely with respect to the maximum number of credit hours that may be transferred from a community college, ranging from fifty-four to no maximum. Based on these findings, a 1993 recommendation by the ASBDCC's Task Force on Enrollment Growth that associate's-degree holders from the state's community colleges be guaranteed admission to a state public university as upper-division students was found to be consistent with national practice.

Tanner, J. M. "The Value of Tracking Students—Gathering Evidence about Their Progress along the Way." Paper presented at the 3rd International Conference for Community College Chairs, Deans, and Other Instructional Leaders, Phoenix, Feb. 23–26, 1994. (ED 368 421)

In response to problems experienced by students from two-year college feeder schools, Brigham Young University (BYU) designed a computer file and transfer matrix screen to automate and standardize the transfer evaluation process. The file contains transcript information on courses for each college providing transfer students, including such information as the course name, department, catalog number, credit hours, and upper- or lower-division status; equivalent BYU course identification; whether credit is accepted by BYU; and whether entry has been validated. This process ensures uniform advising efforts as counselors and transfer students receive a computerized matrix showing how their previous coursework has been evaluated by BYU and a document showing the application of transfer course work to BYU degree requirements. This process has also proved useful in recruiting and information visits to feeder schools. These changes have made a major improvement in relations with transfer students and administrators by making BYU a partner rather than an adversary. Sample transfer matrices, student progress report, and transfer student profile are attached.

Illinois Community College Board. *Articulation Agreements between High Schools, Community Colleges, and Universities.* Springfield: ICCB, 1992. (ED 352 100)

Designed to assist college officials in developing and revising articulation agreements, this report describes specific program articulation efforts between Illinois high schools, community colleges, and public and private universities. Data presented were drawn from a survey of 102 public and private community colleges, which resulted in ninety-four responses identifying forty-five articulation agreements in place among responding institutions. Following an introductory discussion of articulation, the report reviews eleven articulation agreements, providing the names and addresses of contact persons. Finally, the report examines the following features common to many of the articulation agreements described: transfer and articulation agreements as an institutional priority; delineation of admission, program, and other requirements; maintenance of agreements and obligations to inform students; diversity in program options and student services; and support for agreements through educational guarantees of transfer credit.

California Postsecondary Education Commission. *Transfer and Articulation in the 1990s: California in the Larger Picture.* Sacramento: CPEC, 1990. (ED 338 200)

This report puts California's current efforts to find solutions to its problems of transfer and articulation in the broader context of national concerns. Following a brief summary and overview, the paper sets forth a series of conclusions and six recommendations for action by the University of California, California State University, the California Community Colleges, and the commission itself. The paper then describes recent developments in seven states—Arizona, Colorado, Florida, Illinois, Maryland, Texas, and Washington—that are attempting to improve transfer and articulation processes. Next, the paper summarizes research and writing about transfer from a national perspective. The next two parts deal with specially funded efforts to improve transfer and articulation, describing federal and foundation funding and discussing various activities and programs that are being undertaken in California itself, respectively. Three appendices describe the transfer efforts of the University of California and California State University and list grants to research projects from the Organization of the State Higher Education Executive Officers.

Cepeda, R., and Nelson, K. "Transfer: A Plan for the Future." Sacramento: Office of the Chancellor, California Community Colleges. Discussed as Agenda Item 7 at a meeting of the Board of Governors of the California Community Colleges, Sacramento, Nov. 14–15, 1991. (ED 337 225)

California Senate Bill (SB) 121 establishes that a strong transfer function is the responsibility of all three segments of higher education—the California Community Colleges (CCC), the University of California (UC), and the California State University (CSU)—and that each segment must develop transfer agreement programs, discipline-based articulation agreements, transfer centers, and a transfer plan for implementation of provisions of the bill. This report reviews the latest transfer statistics in the state (including systemwide trends and institutional differences), summarizes efforts that have been undertaken to strengthen transfer, discusses planning for the future, and presents an outline of the community college transfer plan for implementation of SB 121. Appendixes provide a review of major provisions of SB 121, a detailed data report on trends in transfer statistics, a review of statewide efforts to improve transfer, and the CCC transfer plan. Components of the CCC plan include improving academic advising, increasing underrepresented student transfer, and increasing opportunities for transfer to private institutions.

American Council on Education, National Center for Academic Achievement and Transfer. *Setting the National Agenda: Academic Achievement and Transfer. A Policy Statement and Background Paper about Transfer Education.* Washington, D.C.: ACE, 1991. (ED 336 138)

This paper is also available from Publications Department T, American Council on Education, One Dupont Circle, Washington, D.C., 20036 for $10.00.

Focusing on the academic dimensions of student transfer from two- to four-year institutions, this report seeks to provide a foundation for institutional and academic policy decisions affecting the transfer experience and student achievement. Part I presents a policy statement on academic achievement and transfer and a nine-point agenda for action. The agenda calls on two- and four-year institutions to establish a firm commitment to transfer, enrich the connection between teaching and transfer, revitalize academic relationships between institutions, manage transfer more effectively, identify and realize transfer goals, inform students fully, issue a clear public call for improved transfer, acknowledge the importance of financial support, and establish firm expectations of transfer students. Suggested activities for implementing each of the points are attached. Part II presents a background paper by James C. Palmer and Judith S. Eaton. The paper begins by examining the implications of transfer education for the mission and values of two- and four-year institutions. After reviewing existing research on student transfer, the paper examines strategies commonly used to improve transfer, including interinstitutional arrangements and special student services. The role of faculty in transfer is discussed next. After stressing the importance of building an empirical base to assess transfer improvement projects, concluding comments review the implications of a reemphasis on transfer. A 116-item bibliography is included.

MATTHEW BURSTEIN is user services coordinator at the ERIC Clearinghouse for Community Colleges in Los Angeles.

INDEX

ORDERING INFORMATION

NEW DIRECTIONS FOR COMMUNITY COLLEGES is a series of paperback books that provides expert assistance to help community colleges meet the challenges of their distinctive and expanding educational mission. Books in the series are published quarterly in Spring, Summer, Fall, and Winter and are available for purchase by subscription and individually.

SUBSCRIPTIONS cost $53.00 for individuals (a savings of 33 percent over single-copy prices) and $89.00 for institutions, agencies, and libraries. Please do not send institutional checks for personal subscriptions. Standing orders are accepted. Prices subject to change. (For subscriptions outside of North America, add $7.00 for shipping via surface mail or $25.00 for air mail. Orders *must be prepaid* in U.S. dollars by check drawn on a U.S. bank or charged to VISA, MasterCard, or American Express.)

SINGLE COPIES cost $20.00 plus shipping (see below) when payment accompanies order. California, New Jersey, New York, and Washington, D.C. residents please include appropriate sales tax. Canadian residents add GST and any local taxes. Billed orders will be charged shipping and handling. No billed shipments to post office boxes. (Orders from outside North America *must be prepaid* in U.S. dollars by check drawn on a U.S. bank or charged to VISA, MasterCard, or American Express.)

SHIPPING (SINGLE COPIES ONLY): $10.00 and under, add $2.50; to $20.00, add $3.50; to $50.00, add $4.50; to $75.00, add $5.50; to $100.00, add $6.50; to $150.00, add $7.50; over $150.00, add $8.50.

DISCOUNTS FOR QUANTITY ORDERS are available. Please write to the address below for information.

ALL ORDERS must include either the name of an individual or an official purchase order number. Please submit your order as follows:
 Subscriptions: specify series and year subscription is to begin
 Single copies: include individual title code (such as CC82)

MAIL ALL ORDERS TO:
 Jossey-Bass Publishers
 350 Sansome Street
 San Francisco, California 94104-1342

FOR SUBSCRIPTION SALES OUTSIDE OF THE UNITED STATES, contact any international subscription agency or Jossey-Bass directly.

OTHER TITLES AVAILABLE IN THE
NEW DIRECTIONS FOR COMMUNITY COLLEGES SERIES
Arthur M. Cohen, Editor-in-Chief
Florence B. Brawer, Associate Editor

CC95   Graduate and Continuing Education for Community College Leaders: What It
        Means Today, James C. Palmer, Stephen G. Katsinas
CC94   Achieving Administrative Diversity, Raymond C. Bowen, Gilbert H. Muller
CC93   Promoting Community Renewal Through Civic Literacy and Service Learning,
        Michael H. Parsons, David C. Lisman
CC92   Curriculum Models for General Education, George Higginbottom,
        Richard M. Roman
CC91   Community Colleges and Proprietary Schools: Conflict or Convergence?
        Darrel A. Clowes, Elizabeth M. Hawthorne
CC90   Portrait of the Rural Community College, Jim Killacky, James R. Valadez
CC89   Gender and Power in the Community College, Barbara K. Townsend
CC88   Assessment and Testing: Myths and Realities, Trudy H. Bers, Mary L. Mittler
CC87   Creating and Maintaining a Diverse Faculty, William B. Harvey, James Valadez
CC86   Relating Curriculum and Transfer, Arthur M. Cohen
CC85   A Practical Guide to Conducting Customized Work Force Training, Sherrie L.
        Kantor
CC84   Changing Managerial Imperatives, Richard L. Alfred, Patricia Carter
CC83   Accreditation of the Two-Year College, Carolyn Prager
CC82   Academic Advising: Organizing and Delivering Services for Student Success,
        Margaret C. King
CC81   Directing General Education Outcomes, Neal A. Raisman
CC80   First Generation Students: Confronting the Cultural Issues, L. Steven Zwerling,
        Howard B. London
CC79   Maintaining Faculty Excellence, Keith Kroll
CC78   Prisoners of Elitism: The Community College's Struggle for Stature,
        Billie Wright Dziech, William R. Vilter
CC77   Critical Thinking: Educational Imperative, Cynthia A. Barnes
CC73   Writing Across the Curriculum in Community Colleges, Linda C. Stanley,
        Joanna Ambron
CC71   The Role of the Learning Resource Center in Instruction, Margaret Holleman
CC70   Developing International Education Programs, Richard K. Greenfield
CC63   Collaborating with High Schools, Janet E. Lieberman
CC59   Issues in Student Assessment, Dorothy Bray, Marcia J. Belcher
CC58   Developing Occupational Programs, Charles R. Doty

UNITED STATES POSTAL SERVICE™

Statement of Ownership, Management, and Circulation
(Required by 39 U.S.C. 3685)

1. Publication Title	2. Publication No.	3. Filing Date
NEW DIRECTIONS FOR COMMUNITY COLLEGES	0 1 9 4 - 3 0 8 1	9/26/96

4. Issue Frequency	5. No. of Issues Published Annually	6. Annual Subscription Price
QUARTERLY	4	$53 - indiv. $89 - instit.

7. Complete Mailing Address of Known Office of Publication *(Street, City, County, State, and ZIP+4) (Not Printer)*

350 SANSOME STREET, SAN FRANCISCO, CA 94104 (SAN FRANCISCO COUNTY)

8. Complete Mailing Address of Headquarters or General Business Office of Publisher *(Not Printer)*

SAME AS ABOVE

9. Full Names and Complete Mailing Addresses of Publisher, Editor, and Managing Editor *(Do Not Leave Blank)*

Publisher *(Name and Complete Mailing Address)*

JOSSEY-BASS INC., PUBLISHERS (ABOVE ADDRESS)

Editor *(Name and Complete Mailing Address)*

ARTHUR COHEN, ERIC CLEARINGHOUSE FOR COMMUNITY COLLEGES, SCHOOL OF EDUCATION, UCLA, 3051 MOORE HALL, 405 HILGARD AVE., LA, CA, 90024-1521

Managing Editor *(Name and Complete Mailing Address)*

NONE

10. Owner *(If owned by a corporation, its name and address must be stated and also immediately thereafter the names and addresses of stockholders owning or holding 1 percent or more of the total amount of stock. If not owned by a corporation, the names and addresses of the individual owners must be given. If owned by a partnership or other unincorporated firm, its name and address as well as that of each individual must be given. If the publication is published by a nonprofit organization, its name and address must be stated.) (Do Not Leave Blank.)*

Full Name	Complete Mailing Address
SIMON & SCHUSTER, INC.	P.O. BOX 1172
	ENGLEWOOD CLIFFS, NJ 07632-1172

11. Known Bondholders, Mortgagees, and Other Security Holders Owning or Holding 1 Percent or More of Total Amount of Bonds, Mortgages, or Other Securities. If none, check here. ☐ None

Full Name	Complete Mailing Address
SAME AS ABOVE	SAME AS ABOVE

12. For completion by nonprofit organizations authorized to mail at special rates. The purpose, function, and nonprofit status of this organization and the exempt status for federal income tax purposes: *(Check one)*
☐ Has Not Changed During Preceding 12 Months
☐ Has Changed During Preceding 12 Months
(If changed, publisher must submit explanation of change with this statement)

PS Form **3526**, October 1994   *(See Instructions on Reverse)*

---

13. Publication Name	14. Issue Date for Circulation Data Below
NEW DIRECTIONS FOR COMMUNITY COLLEGES	SUMMER 1996

15. Extent and Nature of Circulation	Average No. Copies Each Issue During Preceding 12 Months	Actual No. Copies of Single Issue Published Nearest to Filing Date
a. Total No. Copies *(Net Press Run)*	1445	1312
b. Paid and/or Requested Circulation		
(1) Sales Through Dealers and Carriers, Street Vendors, and Counter Sales *(Not Mailed)*	290	245
(2) Paid or Requested Mail Subscriptions *(Include Advertisers' Proof Copies/Exchange Copies)*	812	789
c. Total Paid and/or Requested Circulation *(Sum of 15b(1) and 15b(2))*	1102	1034
d. Free Distribution by Mail *(Samples, Complimentary, and Other Free)*	162	176
e. Free Distribution Outside the Mail *(Carriers or Other Means)*	0	0
f. Total Free Distribution *(Sum of 15d and 15e)*	162	176
g. Total Distribution *(Sum of 15c and 15f)*	1264	1210
h. Copies Not Distributed		
(1) Office Use, Leftovers, Spoiled	181	102
(2) Return from News Agents	0	0
i. Total *(Sum of 15g, 15h(1), and 15h(2))*	1445	1312
Percent Paid and/or Requested Circulation *(15c / 15g x 100)*	87%	85%

16. This Statement of Ownership will be printed in the WINTER 1996 issue of this publication. ☐ Check box if not required to publish.

17. Signature and Title of Editor, Publisher, Business Manager, or Owner   Date 9/26/96

Susan E. Lewis   SUSAN E. LEWIS, PERIODICALS DIRECTOR

I certify that all information furnished on this form is true and complete. I understand that anyone who furnishes false or misleading information on this form or who omits material or information requested on the form may be subject to criminal sanctions *(including fines and imprisonment)* and/or civil sanctions *(including multiple damages and civil penalties)*.

Instructions to Publishers

1. Complete and file one copy of this form with your postmaster on or before October 1, annually. Keep a copy of the completed form for your records.

2. Include in items 10 and 11, in cases where the stockholder or security holder is a trustee, the name of the person or corporation for whom the trustee is acting. Also include the names and addresses of individuals who are stockholders who own or hold 1 percent or more of the total amount of bonds, mortgages, or other securities of the publishing corporation. In item 11, if none, check box. Use blank sheets if more space is required.

3. Be sure to furnish all information called for in item 15, regarding circulation. Free circulation must be shown in items 15d, e, and f.

4. If the publication had second-class authorization as a general or requester publication, this Statement of Ownership, Management, and Circulation must be published; it must be printed in any issue in October or the first printed issue after October, if the publication is not published during October.

5. In item 16, indicate date of the issue in which this Statement of Ownership will be printed.

6. Item 17 must be signed.

Failure to file or publish a statement of ownership may lead to suspension of second-class authorization.

PS Form **3526**, October 1994 *(Reverse)*